Reading for the Gifted Student

Challenging Activities for the Advanced Learner

Written by **Kathryn L. O'Dell**

Illustrations by **Holli Conger**

An imprint of Sterling Children's Books

FLASH KIDS, STERLING, and the distinctive Sterling logo are registered trademarks of
Sterling Publishing Co., Inc.

Published by Sterling Publishing Co., Inc.
387 Park Avenue South, New York, NY 10016
Text and illustrations © 2005 by Flash Kids
Distributed in Canada by Sterling Publishing
c/o Canadian Manda Group, 165 Dufferin Street
Toronto, Ontario, Canada M6K 3H6
Distributed in the United Kingdom by GMC Distribution Services
Castle Place, 166 High Street, Lewes, East Sussex, England BN7 1XU
Distributed in Australia by Capricorn Link (Australia) Pty. Ltd.
P.O. Box 704, Windsor, NSW 2756, Australia

Sterling ISBN 978-1-4114-3427-1

Manufactured in Canada

Lot #:
6 8 10 11 9 7 5
12/14

For information about custom editions, special sales, premium and
corporate purchases, please contact Sterling Special Sales
Department at 800-805-5489 or specialsales@sterlingpublishing.com.

Cover image © Rainer Berg/Getty Images
Cover design and production by Mada Design, Inc

Whether your student has been identified as gifted and talented or is simply a scholastic overachiever, school-assigned activities may not be challenging enough for him or her. To keep your student engaged in learning, it is important to provide reading activities that quench his or her thirst for information and allow opportunities to exercise critical thinking.

This workbook contains much more than typical reading passages and questions; it does not rely on the assumption that a gifted and talented first-grader simply requires second-grade work. Instead, the nearly 200 pages of reading passages, comprehension questions, and creative activities are calibrated to match the average reading level, analytical capacity, and subject interest of this specialized group of learners. Specifically, the vocabulary, sentence structure, and length of passages in this grade 1 workbook are set at levels normally appropriate for grades 2 and 3, but the comprehension skills increase in difficulty as the workbook progresses, starting with grade 1 curriculum standards and working through those associated with grade 2. The passages' topics are primarily nonfiction and present concepts, themes, and issues fundamental to all disciplines, including science, social studies, health, and the arts.

Question formats range from multiple choice and short answer to true or false, fill in the blank, and much more. Also sprinkled throughout the workbook are creative activities that will encourage your student to write a story or draw a picture. Your student may check his or her work against the answer key near the end of the workbook, or you may wish to review it together, since many questions have numerous possible answers.

Reading, writing, and language skills are essential to any student's academic success. By utilizing this workbook, you are providing your gifted learner an opportunity to seek new challenges and experience learning at an advanced level.

Contents

A Is for Airplanes

There are many kinds of airplanes. Some airplanes are very small. They have room for the pilot and only one other person. Some airplanes are very big. These big planes are called jets. More than 500 people can fit on the largest jet.

All airplanes have engines and wings. Planes also have wheels. The wheels come out of the bottom of the plane. They come out when the plane takes off and when it lands.

Today, planes go to almost every part of the world. Small planes can fly and land between mountains. Planes with floats can land on water near very small islands. Jets can fly over oceans to places far away. Airplanes go to many wonderful places!

Answer the questions about the reading.

1. What is a big plane called? _____

2. Who flies a plane? _____

3. What comes out of the bottom of a plane? _____

4. Where do planes with floats land? _____

5. Where do planes go? _____

Mrs. Anderson's Airplane Adventure

The Anderson family is going to Disneyland. To get there, they must fly on an airplane. Mrs. Anderson has never been on a plane. She is afraid to fly. Arnold and Annie have never been on a plane, but they aren't afraid. They want to fly. They tell their mom they will help her. Mr. Anderson tells her "Don't worry, honey." She says, "Okay. I will try to be brave."

The Andersons get on the plane. Arnold and Annie hold their mom's hands when the plane takes off. She is nervous, but she is brave. Soon, the flight attendants bring snacks. The family watches a movie on a small screen over their seats. The pilot tells the passengers to look out the window when they fly over the Grand Canyon.

A few hours later, the plane lands. The Andersons get off the plane. Arnold and Annie want to go to Disneyland. Mr. Anderson wants to go to Disneyland. Mrs. Anderson says, "I don't want to go to Disneyland. I want to get back on the plane. That was fun!"

Number the events in the correct order.

_____ The family watches a movie.

_____ The Andersons get on a plane.

_____ Mrs. Anderson likes to fly.

_____ Mrs. Anderson is afraid to fly.

_____ The Andersons plan a trip to Disneyland.

 # B Is for Birthdays

Some important American holidays celebrate the births of famous people. George Washington was the first president of the United States. His birthday was on February 22, 1732. Abraham Lincoln was the sixteenth president of the United States. His birthday was on February 12, 1809. Today, the third Monday in February is a holiday to honor these men. It's called Presidents' Day.

Martin Luther King, Jr., was a famous leader of the American Civil Rights movement in the 1960s. He was born on January 15, 1929. Today, the third Monday in January is a holiday in the United States. It is a day to remember and honor the wonderful things he did. The holiday is called Martin Luther King Day.

The Fourth of July, or Independence Day, is another holiday. It celebrates a famous birthday, but not for a person. It's the birthday of the United States! On July 4, 1776, the United States became free from Britain and became its own country. Now many people light fireworks to say "Happy birthday, America!"

Use what you learned from the reading to write each person's birthday.
Then draw your own picture and write your birthday.

1.  Happy birthday, Martin Luther King, Jr.!
_____

2.  Happy birthday, George Washington!
_____

3.  Happy birthday, Abraham Lincoln!
_____

4.  Happy birthday to you!
_____

Happy Birthday, Brandon!

Number the pictures in the correct order.

Brandon turns one year old.

Brandon has ten candles on his cake.

Brandon gets a car for his birthday.

Brandon gets a puppy for his eighth birthday.

Brandon is born.

Brandon gets a tricycle for his third birthday.

C Is for Cow

What do you call a group of black and white farm animals that moo? Believe it or not, they are not all cows. The correct name for a group of these animals is cattle. Only females with babies are called cows! Females without babies are called heifers. Males with babies are called bulls. Males used for work are called oxen. Males used for meat are called steer. Babies are called calves. Here are more cattle facts.

- Cattle can weigh up to 2,000 pounds each. That is as much as a small car.
- Cattle can each drink up to 50 gallons of water every day. That is about a bathtub full!
- Cattle eat a lot of grass. Their stomachs have four parts!
- Cows can make about 200,000 glasses of milk in their lifetime.
- Calves can walk a few minutes after they are born.

Write **true** or **false** after each sentence about the reading.

1. Male cattle are called bulls, oxen, or steers. _____

2. Baby cattle are called cows. _____

3. Cows make about 200,000 glasses of milk in their lifetime.

_____

4. Calves can walk soon after they are born. _____

Cattle Call

Circle the best sentence for each picture.

1.

Cattle eat a lot of grass.

Cattle make a lot of milk.

2.

A mother is called a cow.

Calves can walk soon after they are born.

3.

Cattle that work on farms are called oxen.

Cattle can weigh up to 2,000 pounds.

4.

Cattle drink from bathtubs.

Cattle drink up to 50 gallons of water a day.

D Is for Dolls

Circle the items that are shown in the picture.

green dress	blue dress	cows	yellow dress
black hat	pink hat	red hat	blue hat
cell phone	computer	books	umbrella
dolls	teddy bears	red dress	dog

Big Day for a Doll

Daisy Duncan has a doll collection. She has paper dolls. She has rag dolls and plastic dolls. But her favorite doll is one that belonged to her grandmother. The doll is made of porcelain. Her name is Delilah. She is more than 50 years old. She has a very pretty dress. She also has gloves, a hat, and a fancy umbrella.

One day, Daisy brings her doll when she goes to an antique fair with her family. At the fair, different booths sell all kinds of old and valuable items. They sell furniture, artwork, and jewelry. One booth sells antique dolls.

A man working in the doll booth spots Daisy and Delilah. He asks Daisy if he can look at her doll. He says she is in great condition. Her clothes still look new. The paint on her face has few marks or scratches. It is hard to find an old doll that has been cared for so well. He says that Delilah is worth $1,000. He asks, "Would you like to sell your doll?"

Daisy says, "Oh, no! I'm going to keep Delilah, the thousand-dollar doll!"

Answer the questions about the story. Circle the letter of the answer.

1. What is another title for the story?

    a. Daisy's Doll Collection

    b. Daisy's $1,000 Doll

    c. Delilah and Her Doll

2. What does **antique** in paragraph 2 mean?

    a. old

    b. new

    c. expensive

3. What does **condition** in paragraph 3 mean?

    a. the state of something

    b. the price of something

    c. the age of something

4. Why is the doll worth so much money?

    a. It is very pretty.

    b. It has an umbrella.

    c. It is old but in good condition.

E Is for Elephants

Do you know that there are two kinds of elephants? They are the African elephant and the Asian elephant. Both kinds of elephants have long trunks. Both have four legs, four knees, and small tails. But there are a few important differences between the two kinds of elephants.

African Elephant

The African elephant lives in Africa. It can grow to more than 13 feet tall. It has bigger ears than the Asian elephant. It also has longer tusks. The African elephant has a dipped back. That means it curves in. It also has a smooth forehead.

Asian Elephant

The Asian elephant lives in Asia. It is smaller than the African elephant, and it has smaller ears. It has shorter tusks, too. The Asian elephant has an arched back. That means it curves up. It also has two bumps on its forehead.

Next time you see an elephant, look closely. See if you can figure out which kind of elephant it is!

Label the pictures. Write **African Elephant** or **Asian Elephant**.

1.

2.

_____   _____

Elephant Tales

Circle the books that might have information about elephants.

Animals in Africa

All About Monkeys

Asian Animals

Tusks and Trunks

Rivers and Lakes

All About Bicycles

Animals in Zoos

How to Tell Time

Big Animals Around the World

Insects and Reptiles

F Is for Fiji

Fiji is a country in the Pacific Ocean. It is made up of a group of small islands. There are about 330 islands. Most of the people in Fiji live on the two biggest islands. There are many mountains, volcanoes, and tropical forests on the islands. It's hot in Fiji all year.

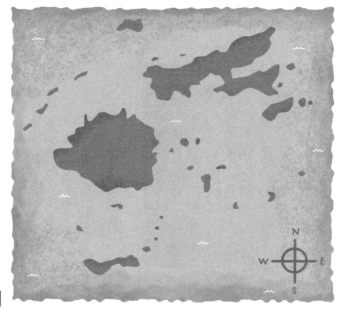

People from all over the world visit Fiji. They swim in the ocean. They enjoy the warm weather and beautiful beaches. They also like to see the tropical forests.

Two islands have large airports for big jets. Many of the other islands have small airports. Some of the islands don't have airports at all. The only way for visitors to get to those islands is by boat!

Answer the questions about the reading.

1. How many islands are in Fiji?_____

2. Why do people visit Fiji?_____

_____

3. How many large airports are there in Fiji?_____

4. How do visitors get to Fiji's smallest islands?_____

5. Would you like to visit Fiji? Why or why not?_____

_____

Flora Goes to Fiji

Dear Frank,

Hello from Fiji! I am here on vacation with my family. We are staying on the biggest island. It is called Viti Levu. On our first day here, we went to a beautiful beach. I saw sea turtles swimming in the ocean. We also hiked in a tropical forest. I took a picture of an iguana and a bright orange bird.

This morning we took a boat to a smaller island. The water is very blue here. The weather is sunny and very hot. I'm sitting under a palm tree and writing postcards.

I hope you're having a good summer. See you next week.

Your friend,
Flora

Place a check next to the things that Flora did.

1. _____ Flora went to the beach.

2. _____ Flora rode in a boat.

3. _____ Flora saw a dolphin.

4. _____ Flora took pictures.

5. _____ Flora caught a bird.

G Is for Greenland

Greenland is the world's largest island. It belongs to the country of Denmark. People on Greenland speak Greenlandic and Danish. Many people in Greenland speak English, too. The capital is a city called Nuuk.

Greenland is one-quarter the size of the United States. It is very big, but not many people live there. That is because most of Greenland is covered with ice. People live only on the parts of the island not covered in ice.

Even in the summer, Greenland is cool. Sometimes it might be warm, but it's never hot. During the summer months, it is light outside during the day and night.

In the wintertime, Greenland is very cold. Most of the time, it's freezing! It stays dark outside both day and night.

Place a check under the word that describes each term from the reading.

	Island	Country	City	Language
1. Greenland				
2. Nuuk				
3. Denmark				
4. Greenlandic				

Warm or Winter Weather?

This was the weather for Nuuk, Greenland, last week.

☀	☀	☁	❄	❄	❄	❄
14°F	12°F	10°F	10°F	7°F	8°F	4°F
Sunday	Monday	Tuesday	Wednesday	Thursday	Friday	Saturday

Use the chart to answer the questions.

1. What was the temperature on Tuesday? _____

2. Which days were sunny? _____

3. Which day was cloudy? _____

4. Which days had snow? _____

_____

5. Do you think this chart shows summer or winter weather? _____

H Is for Hippo

The word **hippopotamus** comes from two Greek words that mean **river horse**. But a river hippopotamus, or hippo, is not much like a horse at all! This huge animal is closer to an elephant in size. It can weigh up to 3,000 pounds. It eats about 130 pounds of fruit, grass, and leaves each day.

River hippos live in Africa. They spend a lot of time in the water. Their webbed toes help them swim. They can keep their large bodies underwater while their eyes, ears, and nostrils peek out into the air. Hippos can also close their ears and nostrils to keep water out.

A baby hippo is called a calf. A calf can weigh 100 pounds when it is born. It can swim right away. A calf rides on its mother's back while she floats in the water. It stays close to her on land. While few animals hunt the huge adult hippos, sometimes crocodiles or lions attack the calves.

Place a check next to each sentence that is true.

1. _____ A hippo is just like a horse.

2. _____ Hippos eat 3,000 pounds of food each day.

3. _____ Hippos can close their ears and nostrils.

4. _____ Lions sometimes attack baby hippos.

5. _____ Baby hippos are very tiny.

Hope Helps Out

Hope's very favorite place in the world is the aquarium near her home. That is where she watches Button and Genny. They are two Nile River hippos. She loves to watch them play underwater. They bounce along the bottom of their tank. They swim in graceful circles. She thinks that they look like huge ballet dancers.

One day in school, Hope's teacher tells the class about hippos. He says that there are fewer hippos every year. Hunters shoot the animals for their skin and teeth. Farmers use the land where hippos live to grow crops. There is less room for the animals.

Hope feels sad. She decides to start a club called Save the Hippos. She sells cookies and lemonade to make money. She asks people in her neighborhood to donate spare change. She collects $50. Her mother helps her find a group that cares for wounded hippos in Africa. Hope sends the money and feels proud.

Draw a line to match words that have the same meaning.

graceful	big
huge	hurt
wounded	smooth
change	jump
bounce	money

I Is for Igloo

An igloo is a house made from blocks of snow. The blocks of snow are put on top of each other. They make a dome. The igloo protects people from cold wind. Heat from the bodies inside keeps the igloo warm.

In the past, many people in very cold places, such as Greenland, used igloos. They usually did not live in the igloos every day, though. They lived in them when they were away from home, on hunting and fishing trips.

There are three kinds of igloos. The smallest igloo can be made in less than ten minutes! Another kind of igloo has one large room that a few people can sleep in. This kind takes more time to build but lasts longer. The third kind of igloo is the biggest. It can have 5 rooms and 20 people can live and sleep in it.

Write the paragraph number (**1**, **2**, or **3**) for each main idea.
Then draw a line to match its supporting detail.

Main Ideas	Supporting Details
_____ kinds of igloos	Igloos are made of blocks of snow.
_____ what an igloo is	The smallest igloos are made quickly.
_____ who lives in igloos	People did not live in igloos every day.

Igloo Ice-o-lation

Color the nouns light blue. Color the verbs dark blue.

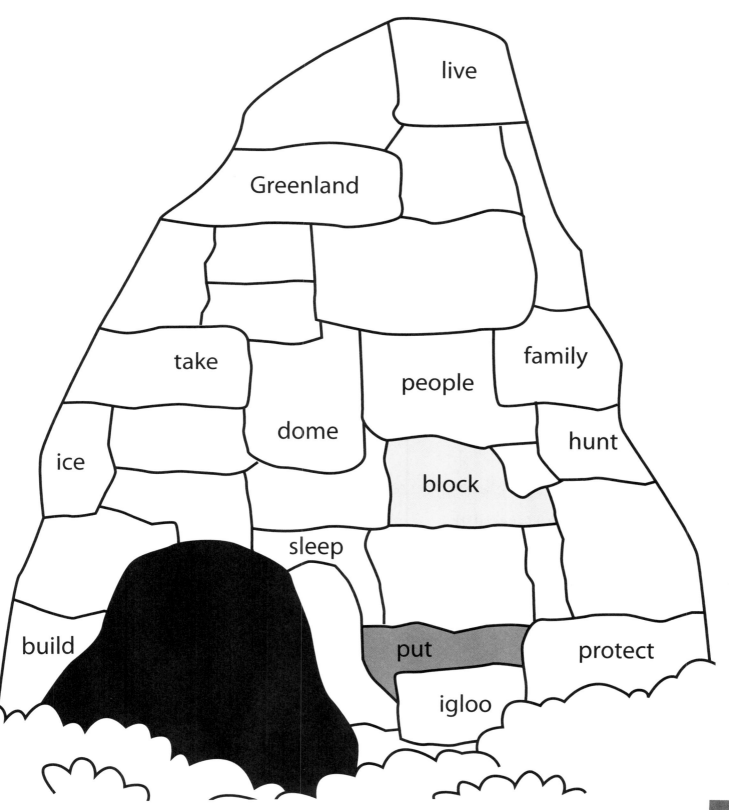

live

Greenland

take

people

family

dome

hunt

ice

block

sleep

build

put

protect

igloo

J Is for Jump Rope

There are many ways to use a jump rope. You can jump rope by yourself. You can jump rope with other people. One person holds each end of the jump rope and swings it, and a third person jumps in the middle. Try these ways to jump rope!

The Basic Jump

Start with the rope behind your feet. Swing the rope over your head and jump when it gets to your feet. Hop over it with both feet at once. See how many times you can do it without missing. When you are ready to challenge yourself, try it on just one foot!

The Criss Cross

Do the Basic Jump, but when the rope is in front of you, cross your arms. Uncross them after you jump.

The Backward Jump

This is the same as the Basic Jump, but in the opposite direction. Begin with the rope in front of your feet. Swing it from front to back over your head.

Answer the questions about the reading. Circle the letter of the answer.

1. What is the purpose of the reading?
   a. to tell someone different ways to jump rope
   b. to show how a jump rope is made

2. For which jump do you swing the opposite direction from the Basic Jump?
   a. The Criss Cross
   b. The Backward Jump

3. How many kinds of jumps does the reading give?
   a. three
   b. four

4. Which jump seems more difficult?
   a. The Basic Jump
   b. The Criss Cross

Jump to It!

Draw jump ropes to match words with the same meaning.

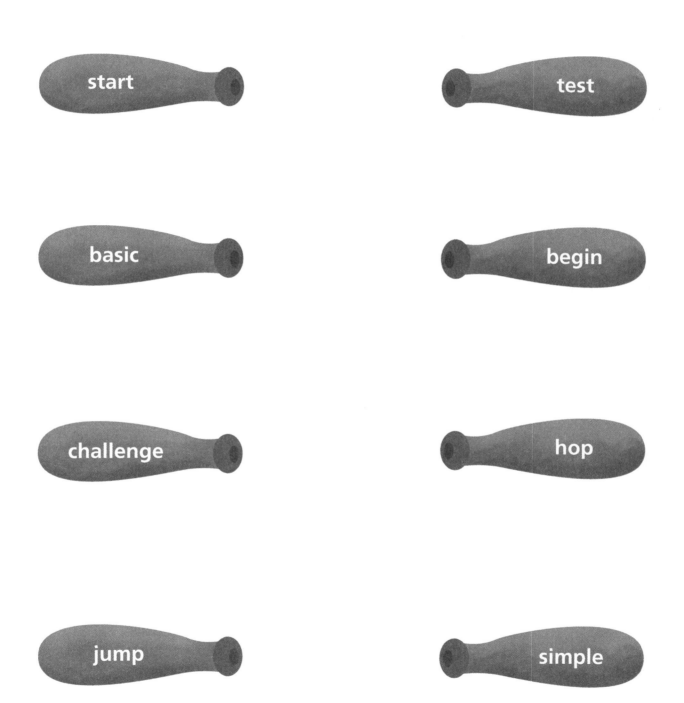

start

test

basic

begin

challenge

hop

jump

simple

K Is for Kaleidoscope

In 1816, a scientist named Sir David Brewster wanted to learn more about light. He made a tube. He put two mirrors along the inside and put two clear circles at one end. Between the circles, he put some beads.

When he looked through the other end of the tube, he saw that the reflection of the beads in the mirrors made pretty designs. As he turned the tube, the beads moved and the designs changed. The patterns were fun to watch. Brewster thought his new invention might make a good toy. He was right! The invention, called a kaleidoscope, quickly became popular with children. Even today, almost 200 years later, kids still enjoy Brewster's simple but interesting toy.

Answer the questions about the reading.

1. What was Brewster trying to study when he made his invention?

_____

2. What part of the kaleidoscope makes reflections?

_____

3. Why did Brewster think his invention would make a good toy?

_____

4. Would you like to play with a kaleidoscope? Why or why not?

_____

A Kaleidoscope of Colors

Look at each word on the left side of the circle.
Find its matching abbreviation on the right side. Color them to match.

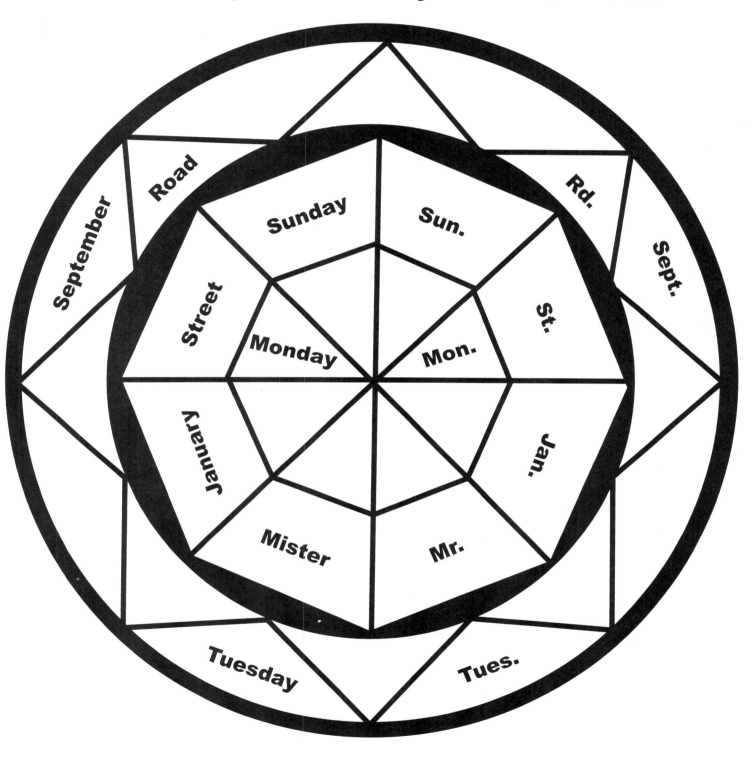

September · Road · Sunday · Sun. · Rd. · Sept. · Street · Monday · Mon. · St. · January · Jan. · Mister · Mr. · Tuesday · Tues.

L Is for Lots of Limes

Sometimes words have more than one meaning. The word **lime** has a few.

A lime is a fruit. It grows on trees. The fruit is usually only a few inches long. The peel is bright green and the inside is light green. It tastes sour. People cook with limes. The juice can be squeezed into a dish to add flavor. There is even a pie made with limes. It's called Key lime pie!

Lime is a color. It is a shade of green that looks like the skin of the lime fruit.

Lime is a mineral. It is found in the earth. Limestone is made with the mineral lime. Limestone is used to make many buildings.

Lime was even the name of a band! The band was popular in the 1980s and played disco music.

Write **M** next to the main idea of the passage.
Write **S** next to the supporting details.

1. _____ There was a band called Lime.

2. _____ Limes are used to make pie.

3. _____ The word **lime** can mean different things.

4. _____ The color lime is bright green.

5. _____ Limes grow on trees.

Lime Time

Ricky's neighbor Martin had a big, strong oak tree in his yard. It was a good tree for climbing. It even had a tree house in it! Ricky had a lime tree in his yard, but it was very small. It was too small to climb. It was much too weak to hold a tree house.

Ricky wished he had a big tree in his yard. He told his parents. His father said, "When life gives you lemons, make lemonade!"

Ricky was confused.

His mother laughed. She said, "He means that if something isn't good, make the best of it!"

Ricky thought about it. He decided to make lime snow cones! He used crushed ice, limes from his lime tree, and sugar to make them. He went to Martin's house to share the treats. Martin invited him to come eat in his tree house! Ricky decided that making the best of it was a great idea.

Complete the chart about the story.

	Ricky's Tree	Martin's Tree
1. Limes		doesn't have limes
2. Climbing	too small to climb	
3. Size	small	
4. Strength		strong
5. Tree house		has a tree house

M Is for Morocco

Morocco is a country in northern Africa. People in Morocco speak Arabic and French. The capital city is Rabat, but it is not the biggest city. The biggest city in Morocco is Casablanca.

Morocco has a king. It has a prime minister, too. A prime minister is similar to a president. The king and the prime minister lead the country together.

Morocco has many mountains and valleys. It has deserts and sand dunes, too. It also has beautiful beaches. The summers in Morocco are hot and dry. The winters are cold and wet.

Moroccan food is spicy. Chicken is very popular. People cook with mint, olives, oranges, and lemons. Many people in Morocco like to drink tea with mint.

Write **true** or **false** after each sentence about the reading.

1. Casablanca is the capital of Morocco. _____

2. Morocco has a king. _____

3. The weather is the same all year in Morocco. _____

4. People in Morocco don't eat chicken. _____

5. Morocco is in the north part of Africa. _____

Melinda's Miserable Vacation

Melinda went to Morocco with her family. Read about her trip.
Read the cause and circle the picture of the effect.

1. It rained all day on Monday.

a.  **b.**

2. Melinda went surfing on Tuesday. She fell off the surfboard.

a. 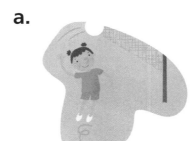 **b.**

3. Melinda ate too much food at a popular restaurant.

a.  **b.**

4. Melinda went hiking in the desert on Thursday. She forgot to bring water.

a.  **b.**

5. Melinda and her family missed their plane home.

a.  **b.**

N Is for Nazca Lines

The Nazca Lines are in the country Peru. They are lines on the ground that form shapes and pictures. The lines were made hundreds of years ago.

Some of the lines make interesting designs. Others make pictures of animals. They show monkeys, spiders, llamas, hummingbirds, sharks, fish, and lizards! This is not a shock. All of these animals live in Peru. They also lived there hundreds of years ago.

The pictures the lines make are very big. Some of them are 400 feet long! It is impossible to see the pictures of the animals when you are on the ground. You can see them only from a plane. It's a mystery how the lines were made. People made the pictures before planes were invented.

Answer the questions about the reading. Circle the answer.

1. What does **ground** in paragraph 1 mean?

    land   crush

2. What does **form** in paragraph 1 mean?

    to make   a shape

3. What does **designs** in paragraph 2 mean?

    patterns   plans

4. What does **shock** in paragraph 2 mean?

    lightning   surprise

5. What does **mystery** mean in paragraph 3?

    a book   unknown

Spider's Secret

One day, hundreds of years ago, a tiny spider was walking on the ground in Peru. She saw some people making huge lines on the ground. They were making interesting patterns. The spider had an idea. She told the people they should shape the lines like giant animals.

The people liked the idea. But they needed help to draw the animals. The spider made a parachute out of her web. She flew above the people. She told the people where to put the lines to make a monkey shape. It worked! Every day she helped the people make different animals. They made a lizard. They made a hummingbird. They even made a spider.

The people couldn't see the animals from the ground, but the spider could. The tiny spider took her friends to see the lines. They loved looking at all of the animals from their web parachutes in the sky.

Only years later, after airplanes were invented, could people fly up and see the animals. Until then, they were the spider's secret.

Answer the questions about the story.

1. Is this a folktale or a mystery?_____

2. Is the main character a monkey or a spider?_____

3. Does the story take place in the past or the present?_____

4. Do lizards or spiders see the animals from the sky?_____

5. Were airplanes invented before or after the spider helped make the lines?_____

O Is for Oh!

There are many sayings with the word **Oh**. Read about some of them.

Oh, yeah.   People say this when they agree with someone.

Oh.   This is another way to say the number **zero**.

Uh-oh!   People say this when they make a mistake or something goes wrong. A mistake can also be called an uh-oh!

Oh, boy!   People say this if they are excited or surprised by something.

Choose the best **Oh** saying to complete each sentence.

1. Mindy: Hi, Jack. What are you doing?

Jack: I'm jumping rope. _____! I just missed!

2. Sue: Look, Mom! I like those kittens.

Mom: You can have one.

Sue: _____! That's great.

3. Larry: What is your phone number?

Kyle: It's seven, five, two, six,_____, three, nine.

4. Linda: This pizza is delicious.

Mia: _____. It's the best pizza I've ever tasted.

Oscar's Big Uh-Oh

Oscar woke up late on Monday morning. He had only fifteen minutes to get ready for school! Quickly, he threw on his clothes. He dashed down the stairs, two at a time, and ran into the kitchen. He poured a bowl of cereal, splashed in some milk, and gobbled it down. On the way to the front door, he grabbed his backpack from the row of hooks by the front door. He sprinted three blocks to the bus stop. Just as he arrived, the bus pulled up. Oscar hopped on and sat down next to his friend Odette.

"I made it!" said Oscar proudly.

"Oh, boy!" said Odette. "I have never seen a backpack like that."

Oscar didn't understand. Then he looked at his lap. Instead of his own backpack, he had grabbed his mother's purse.

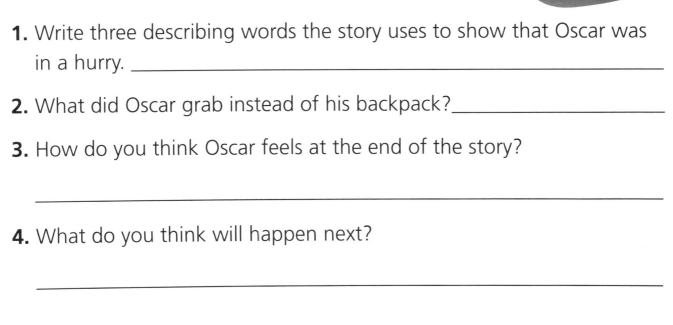

"Uh-oh!" said Oscar. "I think my mom might be looking for this!"

Answer the questions.

1. Write three describing words the story uses to show that Oscar was in a hurry. _____

2. What did Oscar grab instead of his backpack?_____

3. How do you think Oscar feels at the end of the story?

_____

4. What do you think will happen next?

_____

_____

P Is for Pencil

Pencils are the most popular writing instrument in the world. They have been around for hundreds of years. The first pencils were flat pieces of lead. Later, people used long sticks of lead or silver to write. These did little more than make scratches. Then people discovered that the mineral graphite could make dark marks. They began to put long sticks of graphite into wooden tubes. These were the first modern pencils.

The core of a pencil is still called the lead, though it is actually made from graphite. Pencil makers developed a rating system to tell the hardness of the lead in their pencils. Number 1 pencils have the softest lead. They make a very dark mark. Number 4 pencils have hard lead. They make light marks. Most students use number 2 pencils. Look at your pencil. Does it have the number 2 on it?

Number the sentences in the correct order.

_____ People used long metal sticks to write.

_____ People discovered that the mineral graphite could make dark marks.

_____ People wrote with flat pieces of lead.

_____ People put sticks of graphite into wooden tubes.

_____ Pencil makers developed a rating system to tell hardness.

Fun Families!

Match words from the same word family. Draw lines from the pencils to the erasers. Some words won't be used.

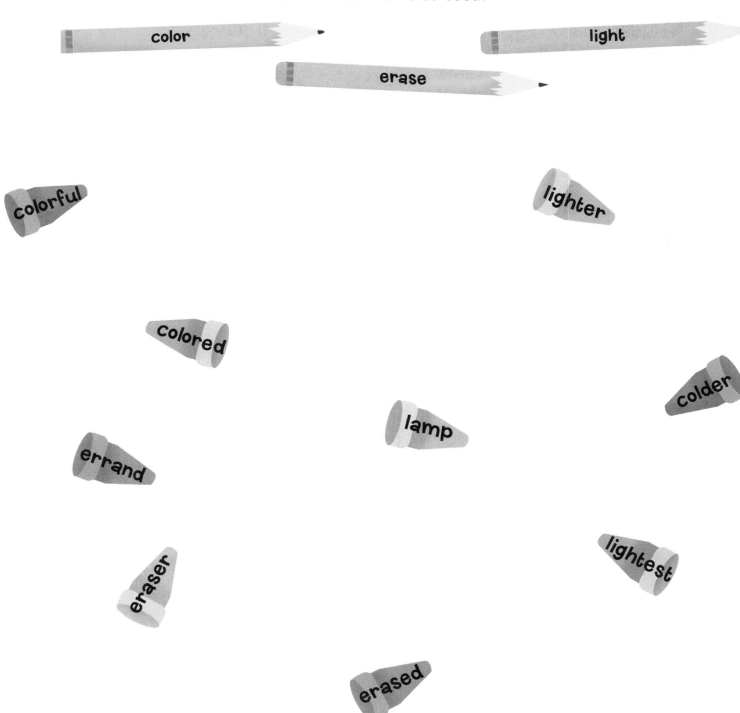

color

light

erase

colorful

lighter

Colored

colder

lamp

errand

lightest

eraser

erased

37

Q Is for Quad

Quad is a prefix that means four. It is used in all kinds of words.

In Sports

A quad is a vehicle that has four big wheels and a motor. A quad is also the name of a ski lift that holds four people. A quadruple is the name of a jump in ice skating. In this jump, the skater turns around four times in the air.

In Music

There was a band in the 1970s and 1980s called The Quads. There were four people in the band. Quad toms are four drums hooked together. They are used in marching bands. Quadraphonic sound is made when four speakers are used at the same time.

In Math and Science

The quadriceps are the four muscles on the front of the thigh. A quadrilateral is a shape with four sides. Quadruplets are four babies born at the same time. A quadruped is an animal that walks on four legs.

Replace the underlined words in the sentences. Use words from the reading.

1. Tom, Rudy, Liv, and Sandra are <u>triplets</u>. _____

2. Tom likes to ride his <u>bicycle</u>. _____

3. Liv is a great ice skater. Her best jump is the <u>half flip</u>.
_____

4. Rudy loves to roller skate. It helps him build his <u>leg muscles</u>.
_____

5. Sandra is in the marching band. She plays the <u>trumpet</u>.

_____

Four of a Kind?

Ned, Luke, Joe, and Peter are brothers. They are quadruplets. They look alike, but they are very different from one another.

Ned is very quiet and shy. He loves to read. He loves mystery books. He also writes stories. He enjoys playing games on the computer. He likes to take the dog, Fluff, for long walks in the park.

Luke is noisy. He listens to loud music. He talks loudly, and sometimes he sings. He loves to play basketball and soccer with his friends. He also likes to cook. He is very messy in the kitchen.

Joe is adventurous. He likes to climb trees and build forts. He likes to play in the snow in the winter. He likes to build snowmen and slide down big hills. In the summer, he likes to swim.

Peter is creative. He loves to paint and draw. He likes to paint pictures of animals. He also likes to ride his bicycle. Sometimes he rides to the art store to buy paints and colored pencils.

Place a check next to what each boy might get for his birthday.

	Ned	Luke	Joe	Peter
1. Paintbrushes and a drawing pad				
2. A cookbook and an MP3 player				
3. A raft and a sled				
4. A computer game and a book				

R Is for Reindeer

Reindeer are rare animals. There are only a few thousand in the world. They live in very cold places like Canada, Norway, Greenland, and Iceland. Their thick hooves help them walk on ice and snow. Their fur keeps them warm in freezing winter.

Adult reindeer weigh between 200 and 400 pounds. They are big, but they can run up to 50 miles per hour. They can also swim. Reindeer travel together in herds. They walk through forests, climb mountains, and swim in rivers.

Answer the questions about the reading. Circle the letter of the answer.

1. How much might a reindeer weigh?
   a. 300 pounds
   b. 800 pounds

2. Where would be the best place to find a reindeer?
   a. a place where it snows a lot
   b. a place where it is often warm

3. What does **rare** mean in this passage?
   a. not common
   b. not cooked

4. How does a reindeer run?
   a. slowly
   b. quickly

Fact or Fiction?

Fact is something that is true. Fiction is something that is not true.
Write **fact** or **fiction** under each picture.

1. Reindeer eat grass.

_____

2. Reindeer can swim.

_____

3. Reindeer can fly.

_____

4. Reindeer live in jungles.

_____

5. Reindeer walk on ice.

_____

S Is for Siamese Cat

Siamese cats are easy to spot. They have very unusual coats. Their fur is mostly white, but there is color on their mouths, noses, ears, paws, lower legs, and tails. The color can be dark blue-gray, light gray, dark brown, or light brown. The color makes the Siamese cats unique. Their eyes are also different from the eyes of other cats. They are shaped like almonds, and they are always blue.

Siamese cats got their name because they are from Thailand. The country Thailand was called Siam before 1945, so the cats got their name from the country Siam.

Siamese cats are very friendly, and they like to be around people. Kittens and adult Siamese cats are very playful. Siamese cats have a very loud meow, and they meow a lot. In fact, people think their meow sounds like a baby crying.

Answer the questions about the reading. Circle the letter of the answer.

1. What is the purpose of the reading?
   a. to tell about Thailand
   b. to give information about Siamese cats

2. What does **coats** in paragraph 1 mean?
   a. fur
   b. jackets

3. What kind of reading is this?
   a. nonfiction: telling about true events
   b. fiction: telling a made-up story

4. What does **unique** in paragraph 1 mean?
   a. like other cats
   b. not like other cats

Opposites Attract!

Antonyms are words that mean the opposite.
Draw a line to match each cat to its opposite collar.

unique

famous

loud

dark

adult

quiet

baby

common

unknown

light

T Is for Twinkle

"Twinkle, Twinkle, Little Star" is a famous nursery rhyme. Jane Taylor wrote the nursery rhyme more than 200 years ago in England. Many children around the world say or sing the nursery rhyme. It has five verses, but most people know only the first verse. Here is the entire nursery rhyme.

Twinkle, twinkle, little star,
How I wonder what you are!
Up above the world so high,
Like a diamond in the sky!

When the blazing sun is gone,
When he nothing shines upon,
Then you show your little light,
Twinkle, twinkle, all the night.

Then the traveler in the dark,
Thanks you for your tiny spark,
He could not see which way to go,
If you did not twinkle so.

In the dark blue sky you keep,
And often through my curtains peep,
For you never shut your eye,
Till the sun is in the sky.

As your bright and tiny spark,
Lights the traveler in the dark,
Though I know not what you are,
Twinkle, twinkle, little star.

1. How old is the nursery rhyme "Twinkle, Twinkle, Little Star"?

_____

2. Who wrote it? _____

_____

3. How many verses does it have?

_____

4. What does **blazing** in verse 2 mean?

_____

5. What does **peep** in verse 4 mean?

_____

Twinkle Time

Janie's little brother Tyler is two years old. He is learning to talk. He makes up new words to his favorite song. It drives Janie crazy. At lunch he sings, "Twinkle, twinkle, little peas." At the park he sings, "Twinkle, twinkle, little swing." In his room he sings, "Twinkle, twinkle, little truck." He sings the song for every new word he learns.

Janie says, "Mom, I can't stand it! Tyler's always singing that song. Make him stop!"

Her mom said, "He's learning new words. Be patient with him."

One night Tyler won't go to sleep. His mom reads him stories. His dad rocks him. Nothing works. Janie decides to sing to him. She sings,

"Twinkle, twinkle, little sleep
Don't make a sound, don't make a peep
I'll count moose or I'll count sheep
I'll keep counting until you fall asleep."

It works! Tyler falls asleep before Janie can start counting. Janie decides that the song isn't so bad after all.

Draw a line to match each story part to the sentence that describes it.

beginning   **Janie makes up her own song.**

middle   **Janie wants Tyler to stop singing.**

end   **Tyler makes up new words to a song.**

U Is for Uno

Uno means "one" in Italian and Spanish. But people use the word in English, too. Here are some examples of things that use the word **uno**.

Businesses

Uno is the name of a bus company in England. Also, the letters UNO are short for the University of New Orleans. They are short for the United Nations Organization, too. Pizzeria Uno is a popular restaurant. There are more than 200 Pizzeria Uno restaurants.

Entertainment

Uno is a card game. It is similar to Crazy Eights. You play it with a special deck of cards. Uno is also an Xbox game that is similar to the card game. Uno was the name of an Italian rock band in the 1970s. It was also the name of a song by a different band in 1999.

People and Things

The Fiat Uno is the name of a small car. Uno is also the nickname of a wrestler. His real name is Rob Conway.

Label each picture with words from the word bank.

| Fiat Uno | University of New Orleans | Uno cards |

1.

2.

3.

_____   _____   _____

I've Got Uno!

Rob and Kate are playing Uno. Number the pictures in the correct order.

Rob finds a game of Uno.

Kate has only one card left.

Rob deals the cards.

Kate wins.

Rob and Kate are bored.

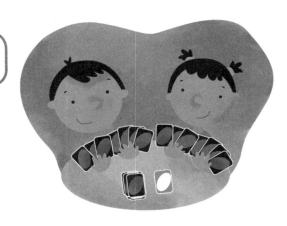

The children begin to play.

V Is for Vancouver

Read the sentences in each pair. Write **C** next to the cause and **E** next to the effect.

1. _____ George Vancouver explored Canada.

_____ A city in Canada was named Vancouver.

2. _____ There is a lot of coal in Vancouver.

_____ Many people moved to Vancouver to work in the coal mines.

3. _____ Many people fish in Vancouver.

_____ There are also lakes and rivers in Vancouver.

4. _____ Many people visit Vancouver on vacation.

_____ Vancouver is a beautiful city. There is a lot to do in Vancouver.

5. _____ Many people in Vancouver speak Chinese and English.

_____ Many street signs in Vancouver are in Chinese and English.

Vincent in Vancouver

Circle all of the action words, or verbs, in the letter.

Hi, Leticia!

I am in Vancouver with my family. It's a big city in Canada. A lot of people live here. It's the third largest city in Canada. There is a lot to do.

We visited the Vancouver Aquarium. I saw a lot of otters and a beluga whale! We also went to Science World. I watched a movie about dinosaurs. Yesterday we drove to the beach. I slid down a huge waterslide at a park! Today we rented bikes. We rode on a beautiful path by the ocean. I am having a great time. See you soon!

Your friend,

Vincent

W Is for Wagon

A wagon is a container with four wheels. It is used to move things. In the past, horses pulled big wagons. People put heavy things in wagons so that they didn't have to carry them. People could ride in the wagons, too. Sometimes wagons had covers to protect people and their things from bad weather.

More than 100 years ago, Antonio Pasin started a company. He named the company Radio Flyer. His company made red toy wagons for children. These wagons are still popular today. The wagons are called Radio Flyer wagons or little red wagons.

Some little red wagons are big enough for one or two small children to ride in. An adult or older child pulls the wagon. Sometimes young children put their toys or dolls inside the wagons and pull them. Today, many little red wagons are still made of wood. Others are made from metal or plastic.

Answer the questions about the reading. Circle the letter of the answer.

1. What is the purpose of the reading?
   a. to tell about wagons
   b. to teach someone how to make a wagon

2. What did Antonio Pasin start?
   a. the first covered wagon
   b. a toy company

3. What pulled covered wagons hundreds of years ago?
   a. people
   b. horses

4. Who pulls little red wagons?
   a. people
   b. horses

Words in Wagons

Write the plurals in the correct wagon. Use the words in the word bank.

company	box	wagon	country
bus	baby	toy	wheel
horse	watch	dress	story

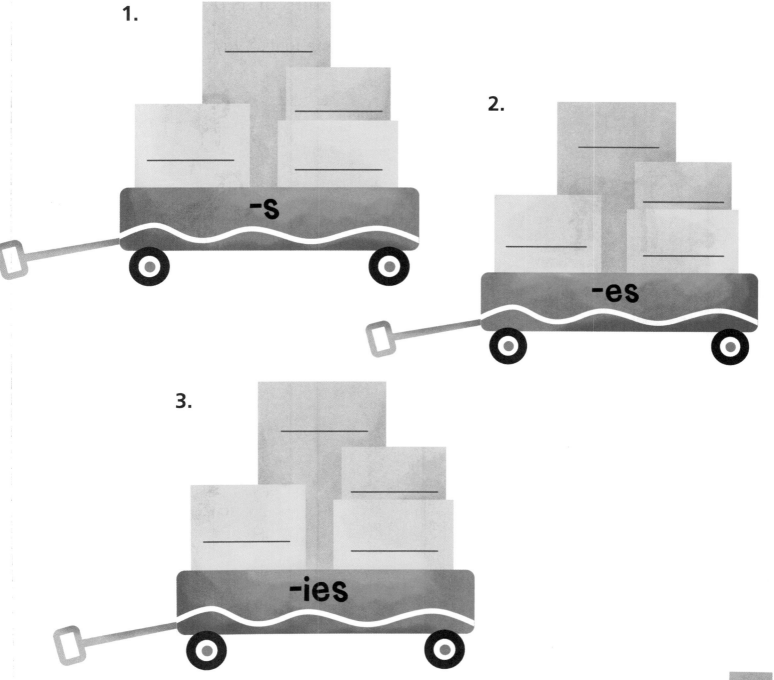

1.

_____

_____

_____

_____

-s

2.

_____

_____

_____

_____

-es

3.

_____

_____

_____

_____

-ies

X Is for X-Rays

    If you have ever broken a bone or been to the dentist, you have probably had an X-ray. X-rays are a form of energy used to make special pictures. These pictures, called radiographs, help doctors look at bones and organs inside the body. They help dentists find cavities inside teeth. X-rays are also useful for veterinarians. Sometimes they can find out what is wrong with a hurt animal by looking at pictures of its bones and organs.

Draw a line to match each picture to its X-ray.

Predict-a-Trip

Look at the X-rays of the people's suitcases. Predict, or guess, what the owner of each suitcase will do on vacation. Use the words in the word bank.

skiing   hiking

camping   swimming

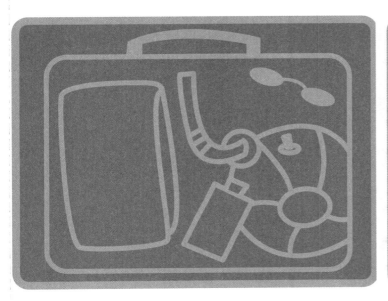

1. _____

2. _____

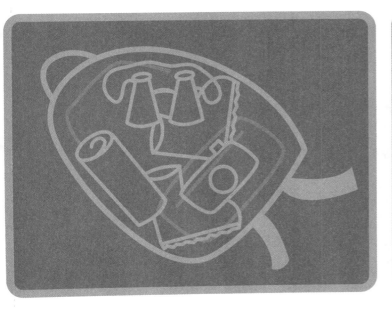

3. _____

4. _____

Y Is for Yaks

Yaks are huge animals that live in Asia. Some yaks are domesticated. That means they live on farms and people take care of them. Other yaks are wild. That means they live on their own. Here are some differences between domesticated and wild yaks:

Wild Yaks	Domesticated Yaks
• They are up to $6\frac{1}{2}$ feet tall. • They are up to 11 feet long. • They weigh up to 1,200 pounds. That's as much as a car! • They are black or brown. • They have long fur that keeps them warm. • They eat grass and plants. • They live on plains and in mountains in China. • There aren't very many wild yaks. They are in danger of dying out.	• They are about half the size of wild yaks. • They are brown or white. • They have long fur that keeps them warm. • They eat grass and plants. • They live on farms in China. • Farmers use them to carry heavy things over the mountains. • Farmers use their milk. • There are about 12 million domesticated yaks.

Circle the correct word in parentheses to complete each sentence.

1. Wild yaks weigh (more / less) than domesticated yaks.

2. Wild yaks are (taller / shorter) than domesticated yaks.

3. Both kinds of yaks have fur that keeps them (cold / warm).

4. Wild yaks and domesticated yaks (eat / don't eat) grass.

5. There are (more / fewer) wild yaks in the world than domesticated yaks.

Yak Attack!

Complete each sentence with the correct homophone, or word that sounds the same.

plains or **planes**

1. Yaks eat grass on the _____ in China.

2. Yaks can't ride on _____ .

way or **weigh**

3. Yaks _____ four times as much as reindeer.

4. Farmers have a _____ to get yak's milk.

their or **there**

5. _____ aren't many wild yaks in the world.

6. Yaks travel with other yaks in _____ herd.

Z Is for Zoo

Zoos have been around for thousands of years. The very first zoos were small collections of wild animals. These zoos belonged to rich and powerful people. Not everyone could visit them.

Public zoos became popular about 500 years ago. During that time, explorers from Europe began to travel to new places in the world. They went to North and South America. They returned with interesting animals no one in Europe had ever seen. These animals were put in cages for people to view. Over time, more animals were added to these collections. They became large places to see and study animals, just like the zoos we visit today.

Answer the questions about the reading. Circle the letter of the answer.

1. What does **collections** in paragraph 1 mean?

  a. groups of things
  b. animals' cages

2. What does **public** in paragraph 2 mean?

  a. private
  b. open to everyone

3. What does **explorers** in paragraph 2 mean?

  a. people who travel to unknown places
  b. people who train animals

4. What does **interesting** in paragraph 2 mean?

  a. exciting
  b. boring

Zoey the Zoologist

Zoey wants to be a zoologist when she grows up. A zoologist studies animals. Zoologists learn about how animals behave. They watch how animals play and hunt. They think about where the animals live and what they eat. The things that zoologists discover help people understand more about animals.

Zoey's favorite book is about Jane Goodall, a zoologist who studies chimpanzees. Dr. Goodall lived with chimps to learn more about their habits. She found that chimps use twigs to catch bugs. This was important because it showed that chimps use tools. People used to think that only humans used tools. Dr. Goodall changed that idea. Zoey hopes that one day she will make her own important animal discovery.

Place a check next to the statements that are true.

1. _____ Jane Goodall is a famous zoologist.

2. _____ Dr. Goodall studies gorillas.

3. _____ Dr. Goodall discovered that chimpanzees use tools.

4. _____ People always knew that monkeys use tools.

5. _____ Zoologists study animals.

Number One Players

Michael Jordan played basketball in the 1980s and 1990s. He was famous for his slam dunks. In fact, he got the nickname "Air Jordan" because he jumped so high in the air.

George Ruth, Jr., was a famous baseball player from 1913 to 1945. People called him "Babe." He was good at hitting home runs.

Christine, or Chris, Evert was one of the best tennis players in the United States from 1972 to 1989. Sometimes she played against one other player. Sometimes she and a partner played against two other players.

Muhammad Ali was a very popular boxer in the 1960s and 1970s. He was a heavyweight boxer. He won so many fights that people called him "The Champ."

Wilma Rudolph was a famous runner from 1956 to 1962. She was the first American woman to win three Olympic gold medals. Her nickname was "The Tennessee Tornado" because she was from Tennessee.

Use the reading to complete the chart.

Name	Nickname	Sport	Years Played
1. Michael Jordan			1980s, 1990s
2. George Ruth, Jr.	Babe		
3. Christine Evert	Chris		
4. Muhammad Ali		boxing	
5. Wilma Rudolph		running	1956–1962

Amazing Athletes

Draw what happened first.

1.

He hit the ball.   He ran to first base.

2.

I stood on the diving board.   I jumped in the water.

3.

She started the race.   She finished the race.

Tea for Two

"Tea for Two" is the name of a famous song. It was first heard in a musical play called *No, No, Nanette*. Vincent Youmans and Irving Caesar wrote the song. The most famous part says, "Just tea for two and two for tea, just me for you and you for me."

In 1950, the play *No, No, Nanette* was made into a movie called *Tea for Two*. The movie starred a famous actress named Doris Day. In the movie, she sang the song "Tea for Two." This helped make the song known to people who had never seen the play.

Many people still like the song today. There are stores and restaurants named after it. For example, there is an online store called Tea for Two. It sells fancy silver teapots and cups. There is a restaurant in New York called Tea for Two. It has tea, but also serves Italian food!

Write **true** or **false** after each statement about the reading.

1. *Tea for Two* is the name of a song, a movie, a store, and a restaurant.

_____

2. Vincent Youmans sang "Tea for Two." _____

3. Doris Day was a movie star and a singer. _____

4. "Tea for Two" isn't popular today. _____

5. The restaurant Tea for Two is in London. _____

Tea Time

Nelly wanted to have a tea party. She decided to have the party on Saturday, March 3. She made invitations for her friends. She wrote what time the party would start and where it would be held. She asked her friends to call her cell phone at 555-2134 to tell her if they could come.

She invited 12 friends, but only 10 came to the party. The party was from 1:00 to 3:00 PM. It was at Pine Park. They sat at a long picnic table in the park. They drank tea and ate cookies. Her mom and older sister had helped her make the tea and cookies. After they ate, Nelly and her friends played games in the park.

Complete Nelly's tea party invitation.

You're Invited

What: _____

Day: _____

Time: _____

Where: _____

Call: _____

Bicycle or Tricycle?

Did you ride a tricycle when you were little? A tricycle is like a bicycle, but it has three wheels. It's called a tricycle because **tri-** means "three." The three wheels make a tricycle easier to balance than a bicycle. For this reason, children usually learn to ride tricycles before they ride bicycles.

Tricycles were not always for children. The first tricycles were for adults. They were invented more than 200 years ago. Today, most tricycles have one big tire in front and two small ones in back. Others have two wheels in front and one in the back.

The world's biggest tricycle took more than three years to build. It was 37 feet long and 41 feet tall! The tricycle weighed about three tons.

Answer the questions about the reading.

1. What does **tri-** mean?

   a. three

   b. two

2. When were tricycles invented?

   a. about 100 years ago

   b. about 200 years ago

3. Do all tricycles have one wheel in front and two in the back?

   a. yes

   b. no

4. How long was the biggest tricycle?

   a. 41 feet

   b. 37 feet

5. Why do most children learn to ride tricycles before they ride bicycles?

   a. Tricycles are easier to balance.

   b. Tricycles are more fun.

Word Wheels

Put the words from the word bank in the correct wheel. The first one is done for you.

small	tricycle	move	wheel
work	ride	big	tall
learn	children	easy	tire

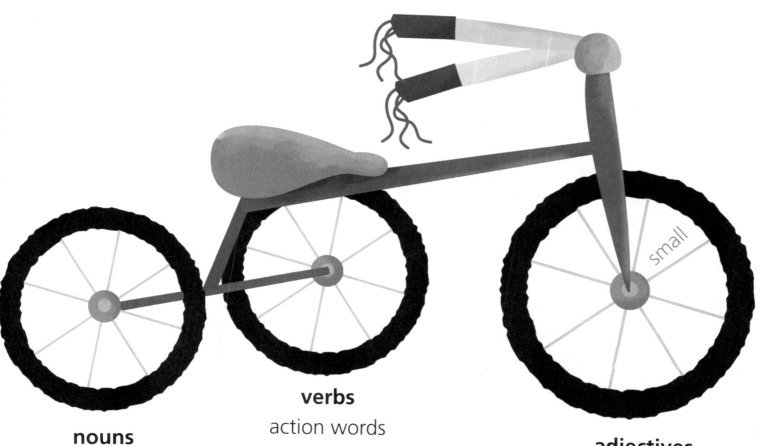

small

nouns
people, places,
or things

verbs
action words

adjectives
describing
words

Four-Star Films

Katia's Movie Mania

Welcome! My name is Katia. I love movies. These are my favorites. I gave them all four stars!

Finding Nemo

This movie is about a fish. His name is Nemo. Nemo doesn't go to school one day. He gets into trouble. His father goes to find him. There are a lot of adventures in this movie. There are even sharks and jellyfish!

The Wizard of Oz

This is an old movie. My mom and dad watched it when they were little. It is about a girl named Dorothy. During a tornado she gets lost in the land of Oz. She tries to get home. She meets a scarecrow, a lion, and a tin man on the way!

Shrek

I love the Shrek movies. They are about an ogre. He has many adventures. There are three different movies about him: Shrek 1, Shrek 2, and Shrek the Third. Shrek 1 is my favorite. He rescues Princess Fiona in it.

1. Which movie's main character is a person?_____

2. Which movie's setting is in the ocean?_____

3. Which movie is about a father and a son?_____

4. Which one has three different movies?_____

5. What is your favorite movie?_____

Rate It!

Draw a line to match each group of stars and the phrase it matches.
Then write the title of a movie you've seen that matches each rating.

Bad. I didn't like it.

_____

Fantastic.
It's my favorite movie.

_____

Okay. It was good,
but not great.

_____

Terrible. I hated it!

_____

Great. I really liked it.

_____

Five-Minute Fun

Do you have a few extra minutes? There are many things you can do in five minutes. Here are ten ideas.

1. Make a sandwich.

2. Run around the block.

3. Use the Internet to learn to say "hello" in another language.

4. Read a picture book.

5. Make up a story. Tell it to a friend.

6. Draw a picture.

7. Write words that start with the first letter of your name. How many can you write in five minutes?

8. Play with your pet.

9. Clean your desk.

10. Listen to your favorite song.

Answer the questions about the list. Write the number of the idea.

1. Which idea includes food? _____

2. Which idea is an art activity? _____

3. Which idea includes an animal? _____

4. Which idea uses a computer? _____

5. Which idea is your favorite? _____

Word Wiz

1. Write five words that start with **T**.

_____, _____,

_____, _____,

_____

tiger
pig
pan
wait
huge

2. Write five words that end with **G**.

_____, _____,

_____, _____,

_____

3. Write five words that rhyme with **can**.

_____, _____, _____,

_____, _____

4. Write five words that rhyme with **late**.

_____, _____, _____,

_____, _____

5. Write five words that mean "big."

_____, _____, _____,

_____, _____

Six Flags

Six Flags theme parks are popular amusement parks. There are 22 Six Flags theme parks. Most of them are in the United States, but there is one in Canada and one in Mexico.

The first Six Flags theme park opened in 1961 in Texas. It's called Six Flags Over Texas. In 1961, tickets cost $2.75 for adults and $2.25 for children. It cost 50¢ to park a car. Hamburgers were 35¢, and sodas were 10¢. There were about 20 rides, shows, and exhibits.

Today, tickets for Six Flags Over Texas cost $47 for adults and $29.99 for children. It costs $15 to park a car. A hamburger costs about $5, and sodas are about $2. There is a lot more to eat in Six Flags Over Texas today. There are more than 20 places to eat in the park. There are also more than 100 rides, shows, and exhibits.

Use the reading to complete the chart about Six Flags Over Texas.

	In 1961	Today
1. Tickets for adults	$2.75	
2. Tickets for children		
3. Parking		
4. A hamburger and a soda		
5. Number of rides, shows, and exhibits		More than 100

Sam and His Six Sisters

Sam Silva has six sisters. He has three older sisters and three younger sisters. One day, they all went to Six Flags. Sam wanted to ride the biggest roller coaster. His sister Sue wanted to ride the teacup ride. "Let's vote," said Sue. His sisters all voted for the teacup ride. Sam voted for the roller coaster. "Six to one," said Sue. They rode the teacups.

Sam wanted to go on a waterslide. His sister Sheila wanted to watch a music show. "Let's vote," said Sheila. His sisters all voted for the show. Sam voted for the waterslide. "Six to one," said Sheila. They went to the show.

At lunch, Sam wanted to eat hamburgers and fries. His sister Sarah wanted to have pizza. "Let's vote," said Sarah. His sisters all voted for pizza. Sam voted for hamburgers. "Six to one," said Sarah. They had pizza.

After lunch, their parents wanted to go home. Sam wanted to stay. "Let's vote," said Sam. His parents voted to go home. Sam and his sisters voted to stay. Sam smiled. "Seven to two," he said. They stayed. "Let's go ride a roller coaster," said Sam. "Okay!" said his sisters.

Number the pictures in the correct order.

The Seven Wonders of the Modern World

Wonder	Description	Country	Date Started	Date Finished
Chunnel	an underwater train tunnel	between France and England	1987	1991
CN Tower	a radio and TV tower	Canada	1973	1976
Itaipu Dam	a dam in the Paraná River	between Brazil and Paraguay	1975	1982
Delta Works	constructions, including dams, that protect land from the ocean	Netherlands	1950	1997
Golden Gate Bridge	a $1\frac{1}{2}$-mile-long bridge in San Francisco	the United States	1933	1937
Empire State Building	a 102-story skyscraper in New York	the United States	1930	1931
Panama Canal	a canal that connects the Atlantic Ocean to the Pacific Ocean	Panama	1880	1914

Use the chart to answer the questions.

1. Which Wonder goes over water?_____

2. Which one took the longest to build? _____

3. Which Wonders are between two countries?_____

_____

4. Which Wonder connects two oceans? _____

5. Which Wonders are not right near water? _____

_____

The Seven Wonders of the Natural World

Nancy Nevin and her family wanted to visit the seven natural wonders. They decided to visit one a year every year.

When Nancy was four years old, the Nevins visited the Northern Lights in Alaska. These are colorful lights that appear in the sky in northern parts of the world.

When Nancy was five, her family went to the Grand Canyon. They went on a raft ride down a river in the canyon. It was very hot.

The next year, the Nevins went to Mount Everest. They climbed only partway up the mountain.

When Nancy was seven, she and her family visited Victoria Falls in Africa. The waterfalls were incredible. It was Nancy's favorite trip.

This year, Nancy is eight. She will go with her family to Rio de Janeiro, Brazil. It is one of the most famous beaches in the world.

Next year, the Nevins will go to Paricutín Volcano in Mexico. After that, they will dive at the Great Barrier Reef in Australia. Then they will have seen all Seven Wonders of the Natural World!

Answer the questions about the story.

1. How many years will it take the Nevins family to visit the natural wonders of the world?_____

2. How old was Nancy when she visited the Grand Canyon?_____

3. How old was Nancy when she saw Mount Everest?_____

4. What country will Nancy visit when she sees a volcano?_____

5. How old will Nancy be when she visits Australia?_____

Magic 8

Abe Bookman invented the **Magic 8-Ball** in 1946. It is a plastic ball with the number 8 on top. On the bottom is a window. Inside is a die. The die has 20 sides. Each side has words on it. You ask the Magic 8-Ball a question. Then you flip it over and look at the answers. Here are the possible answers:

- As I see it, yes
- Ask again later
- Better not tell you now
- Cannot predict now
- Concentrate and ask again
- Don't count on it
- It is certain
- It is decidedly so
- Most likely
- My reply is no

- My sources say no
- Outlook good
- Outlook not so good
- Reply hazy, try again
- Signs point to yes
- Very doubtful
- Without a doubt
- Yes
- Yes - definitely
- You may rely on it

Follow the directions.

1. Circle the answers that mean "yes."

2. Underline the answers that mean "no."

3. Place a check mark next to the answers that mean neither "yes" nor "no."

4. Put an X above the name of the inventor.

5. Draw a wavy line under the name of the toy.

Decisions, Decisions

Carson asked his Magic 8-Ball questions. Then he did what the Magic 8-Ball said. Match each question and answer to his action.

Question: Should I study for my math test?

Answer: It is certain.

Question: Should I bring an umbrella to school?

Answer: Without a doubt.

Question: Should I eat a candy bar?

Answer: My reply is no.

Question: Is it time for bed?

Answer: Signs point to yes.

Nine Lives

It is sometimes said that cats have nine lives. This is not really true. People probably started saying this because cats can escape accidents that would hurt or kill other animals. For example, a cat might fall out of a high window and land without injury. How is this possible? If you have ever dropped something heavy, you know that heavy objects fall hard and fast. Cats are small and light. They don't fall as quickly or as hard as people or large animals. Sometimes they spread their legs out as they fall. This creates an umbrella shape that slows them down even more. Cats also have a very good sense of balance. They use this sense to turn themselves in midair so that they land on all four paws. All of these things work together to help many cats survive dangerous falls. Still, it's not a good idea to let your cat play near an open window!

Write **true** or **false** after each statement about the reading.

1. Cats have nine lives. _____

2. Cats fall slowly because they are small and light. _____

3. Cats can use their legs to make an umbrella shape. _____

4. Cats have a terrible sense of balance. _____

5. It's a good idea to throw your cat out the window. _____

Here Kitty, Kitty

Circle the nine cats that are the same.

Difficult Decathlons

A decathlon is a competition. It has ten events.
The events are:
100-meter run: Athletes run 100 meters.
400-meter run: Athletes run 400 meters.
1,500-meter run: Athletes run 1,500 meters.
110-meter hurdles: Athletes run 110 meters.
They have to jump over hurdles as they run.
Javelin throw: Athletes throw a long, thin pole.
Discus throw: Athletes throw a heavy metal disc.
Shot put: Athletes throw a heavy metal ball.
Long jump: Athletes jump into a sand pit.
The person who jumps the longest distance wins this event.
High jump: Athletes jump over a metal bar. The bar keeps getting higher.
Pole vault: Athletes use a long pole to jump over a bar.

Write the answers on the lines.

1. In these events, athletes throw something.

_____

_____

2. In these events, athletes jump.

_____

_____

3. In these events, athletes run.

_____

_____

Time for Ten

Write ten words using any of these letters.

DECATHLON

1. _____
2. _____
3. _____
4. _____
5. _____
6. _____
7. _____
8. _____
9. _____
10. _____

Shoelace Fun

Here are 11 things you can do with shoelaces.

1. Learn how to tie knots. Practice with a shoelace. You can find directions for tying knots on the Internet.
2. Buy colorful shoelaces. Use them as ribbons on a gift to a friend.
3. Tie several shoelaces together. Use them as a jump rope.
4. Put beads on a colorful shoelace and make a necklace.
5. Decorate white shoelaces with fabric paint.
6. Tie a few shoelaces together. Tie this around a few books. You can carry your books with the shoelace.
7. Sew a shoelace inside each side of your hat. Now you can tie the shoelaces under your chin to keep your hat on!
8. Glue colorful shoelaces around an old pot. Now you have a pretty planter.
9. Tie a few shoelaces together to make a belt.
10. Decorate a white shoelace with markers. Cut the lace in half to make two friendship bracelets.
11. Learn different ways to tie your shoes. You can find directions on the Internet. Tie your shoes a different way each day of the week.

Answer the questions about the list. Write the number of the activity.

1. Which activities include making jewelry? _____ and _____

2. Which activity involves sewing? _____

3. Which activity do you need paint for? _____

4. In which activities do you need the Internet? _____ and _____

5. Which activity do you want to try? _____

A Messy Mission

Circle the 11 things that Lydia has on her art table.

paper	a notebook	a jump rope	shoelaces
ribbon	markers	beads	glue
a pot	a computer	a book	a box
a hat	a pencil	a bracelet	scissors

A Dime a Dozen

A dozen is a group of 12. There are many things that come in groups of 12. Eggs are usually sold in dozens. You can also buy a dozen donuts. A dozen roses is a popular gift. Pencils are often sold in groups of 12, too. You can buy a box of one dozen, two dozen, and even six dozen pencils!

But a dozen doesn't always mean exactly 12. For example, a baker's dozen is 13. It means the baker added an extra one to the dozen, just in case! Also, people sometimes use the word dozen to mean a few of something. Someone might say, "I have dozens of chores to do!" That doesn't mean they have two or three dozen chores. It just means they have a lot of chores.

You might have heard the saying "cheaper by the dozen." This means that things sold in groups are less expensive than those sold one by one. This saying is the title of a popular book and movie about a family with 12 children.

Write **true** or **false** after each sentence about the reading.

1. You can buy eggs, pencils, roses, and donuts by the dozen.

_____

2. A baker's dozen is 13. _____

3. There are usually 13 eggs in a carton. _____

4. A dozen always means exactly 12. _____

5. Things sold in dozens are very expensive. _____

Super Stories

Look at the pictures from a newspaper. Underline the best headline for each one.

1.

A Chicken Eats a Dozen Donuts
A Chicken Lays a Dozen Eggs
A Chicken Gets a Dozen Roses

2.

Dan's Dozen Dogs
Dan's Parents
Dan's Dozens of Cousins

3.

A Baker's Dozen
A Baker Makes a Cake
A Baker Drops a Cake

4.

Martha's Birthday Surprise
Martha Gets 12 Donuts
Martha and Her Chicken

Unlucky 13?

Many people around the world think 13 is an unlucky number. Some hotels don't have a 13th floor. They think some customers will be afraid to stay there. In those hotels, the 14th story comes right after the 12th story! Hotels also don't have rooms with the number 13 on them. Some airplanes skip 13 when they number rows of seats.

Friday the 13th is considered an unlucky day in the United States and many other countries. Some people think bad things will happen on this day. This is called a superstition. There isn't any proof that bad things will actually happen. In fact, sometimes good things happen! In 2006, the 13th book in the popular series A Series of Unfortunate Events went on sale on Friday the 13th.

Draw lines to match the synonyms, or words that mean the same thing.

unlucky	belief
story	leave out
superstition	floor
popular	not lucky
skip	well-liked

Freaky Friday?

It's Friday the 13th and Frida is afraid. She thinks that something bad is going to happen. On her way to school, she sees her best friend, Kate. They walk to school together. They laugh and have fun. At school, Frida gets her spelling test back. She got an A! She plays soccer at recess, and her team wins. For lunch she has her favorite meal—pizza! Her friend Don gives her a chocolate brownie for dessert.

On her way home from school, she finds five dollars on the sidewalk. At home, her father tells her she doesn't have to do her chores because her brother did them for her. Then her mom says, "We're going to watch a movie!" Her mom makes popcorn. The movie is great. Frida decides that Friday the 13th is a very lucky day!

Number the events in the correct order.

Blue Butterflies

Morpho butterflies are very special. They are bigger than regular butterflies. They are at least three inches from wing to wing. Some Morpho butterflies are eight inches wide! They shine like metal. The most common Morpho butterfly is blue. Some Morpho butterflies are green, and some are white. There's even a Sunset Morpho butterfly. It is orange and red.

Morpho butterflies are found in South America, Central America, and Mexico. Morpho butterflies live in shady jungles and forests. Sometimes they fly to open areas where they can warm up in the sun.

Like other butterflies, they start as caterpillars and make a cocoon. Once they turn into butterflies, they live only about three months. They eat juice from fruit. They usually get juice from fruit that is on the ground.

Answer the questions about the reading. Circle the letter of the answer.

1. How wide are Morpho butterflies?

    a. 3 to 8 inches

    b. less than 3 inches

2. What colors can Morpho butterflies be?

    a. only blue

    b. blue, green, white, orange, and red

3. What does **shady** in paragraph 2 mean?

    a. out of the sun

    b. in the sun

4. How long do Morpho butterflies live?

    a. a year

    b. for about three months

Barbara Binken and the Blueberry Pie

Number the pictures in the correct order.

Bluegrass Tunes

Bluegrass music started in the United States in the 1940s. It grew out of a lot of different kinds of music. There are many different instruments in a bluegrass band. Read about some below.

> **Banjo:** This is a string instrument. The strings go over a circle that looks like a drum.
>
> **Harmonica:** This is a small rectangle with holes. You blow in and out to play it.
>
> **Mandolin:** This is a string instrument. The strings go over a wood part that is shaped like a pear.
>
> **Bass:** This like a violin, but it is very big. It's so big you have to stand up to play it.
>
> **Washboard:** A washboard is a board that people used to wash clothes with. It has a wooden frame. The center is metal. People play this as a musical instrument. They move their fingers over the metal to make a sound.

Label each instrument.

1. _____

2. _____

3. _____

4. _____

5. _____

Writing the Blues

1. Write four words that start
with **bl**.

_____blue_____,

_____,

_____,

_____

2. Write three words that end in **ue**.

_____,

_____,

_____

3. Write four things that can be
the color blue.

_____,

_____,

_____,

_____

4. Write three words that
have the word **blue** in them.

_____,

_____,

_____

5. Write five words that rhyme
with **blue**.

_____,

_____,

_____,

_____,

_____

A Red Velvet Recipe

Use the words from the word bank to complete the recipe.

red   oven   eggs   stir   pan

Red Velvet Cake

Ingredients:
1 ½ cups of oil
1 ½ cups of sugar
2 _____
1 cup of milk
1 teaspoon of vanilla

20 drops of _____ food coloring
2 ½ cups of flour
1 teaspoon of baking soda
¼ teaspoon of salt

Directions:
Put the oil, sugar, and eggs in a bowl. Stir. Add the milk, vanilla, and food coloring. _____ again. Then add the flour, baking soda, and salt. Stir again. Put it in a rectangular _____. Put the pan in an _____ at 350 degrees. Bake for 40 minutes. Then let it cool. Add frosting, if you want.

Rita's Red-Letter Day

I had a great day yesterday. It was Saturday. My friend Ron called. He invited me to an amusement park. We got on a lot of rides in the morning. Then we went to a music show. It was a bluegrass band. They sang fun songs. We got on a few more rides, and then we had lunch. I ordered a hamburger and a soda. I also got a red velvet cake for dessert. Ron had a hamburger, an orange juice, and a piece of blueberry pie.

After lunch, we went to the Rain Forest Funhouse in the amusement park. I saw a blue Morpho butterfly. We rode on a rain-forest waterslide. Then we saw a rain-forest animal parade!

I fell asleep in the car. I went to bed as soon as I got home. It was an hour before my usual bedtime, but I didn't mind. It was a red-letter day.

Answer the questions about the story. Circle the letter of the answer.

1. Who is the narrator?
  a. Ron
  b. Rita

2. What is the purpose of the story?
  a. to give directions
  b. to entertain

3. What is the main idea of the story?
  a. Rita had a good day.
  b. There are many things to do at an amusement park.

4. What does **I didn't mind** in paragraph 3 mean?
  a. I'm mad about it.
  b. It didn't bother me.

Say it!

A red-letter day means that a day is really good or special. This saying started hundreds of years ago. People would write holidays in red on church calendars. They started calling these special days red-letter days because they were in red print.

Heartfelt Holiday

Valentine's Day is on February 14. It is a day to celebrate love and friendship. People give each other cards and small gifts. Popular gifts are chocolates and flowers. A dozen red roses is a very common gift. Red and pink are Valentine's Day colors. A heart is a symbol of this day. Many cards are decorated with red and pink hearts.

Years ago, people made Valentine's Day cards. They wrote notes by hand. Today, some people still do that, but many people buy cards. It is one of the biggest days for giving cards. About 1 billion people around the world send cards on Valentine's Day!

Many countries celebrate Valentine's Day on February 14. But some countries have a similar holiday on other days of the year. In Colombia, Love and Friendship Day is on the third Friday and Saturday in September. In Brazil, Girlfriend/Boyfriend Day is on June 12. In Argentina, Friend's Day is on July 20. In South Korea, Pepero Day is on November 11. It gets its name from a popular candy called Pepero!

Draw a line to match each country to the holiday.
Then match the holiday to the month when it is celebrated.

the United States	Friend's Day	July
Colombia	Girlfriend/Boyfriend Day	November
Brazil	Love and Friendship Day	September
Argentina	Pepero Day	June
South Korea	Valentine's Day	February

A Valentine Poem

Read the first lines of the poem. Then fill in the blanks with your own words.

Roses are red,

Violets are blue,

I've never known a valentine nicer than you.

Roses are _____,

Violets are _____,

_____

_____ are _____

_____ are _____

_____

Great! I'm Green!

Green is a color everywhere in nature. Most trees and plants are green. There are also many animals that are green. Their green color helps them blend in with plants and trees. This is called camouflage. It helps protect them from their enemies. Their enemies cannot see them because they are the same color as the leaves nearby. Their enemies may go right by them.

Many reptiles are green, such as lizards, turtles, and snakes. Toads and frogs are green amphibians. Some insects are green, too. Praying mantis and caterpillars are examples of green insects. Even fish can be green, such as some pike. They blend in with green plants in the ocean. There is even a fish called the green-light tetra!

The next time you walk by a green, leafy plant or tree, look closely. There might be a green animal hiding nearby!

Complete the chart with green animals from the reading.

Amphibians	Reptiles	Fish	Insects
_____ _____	_____ _____ _____	_____ _____	_____ _____

Jack the Jealous Giraffe

Jack the giraffe lives in the African grasslands. He loves eating leaves. His favorite color is green. One day, he sees a green crocodile sitting in the sun. He is jealous of the crocodile's green skin. He decides he wants to be green.

He starts eating lots and lots of green leaves. He eats them all day and all night. He doesn't get green. He just gets bigger. He rolls around in grass, hoping to turn green. It doesn't work. He just gets dirty.

One day he walks around in the grasslands. The grass is brown and tall. He hears some hyenas coming. They are loud, and they are hungry. He is very scared. He crouches down in the brown grass. The hyenas don't see him. His brown spots blend in with the grass and camouflage him. The hyenas leave and he is safe. Now he is happy that he is not green!

Draw a line from each cause to its effect.

Cause

Jack sees a green crocodile.

He eats green leaves.

He rolls in the grass.

He hears hyenas.

His brown spots camouflage him in the grass.

Effect

He is scared.

He gets bigger.

He is safe and happy that he's not green.

He wants to be green.

He gets dirty.

Good Greenhouses

A greenhouse is a type of building used to grow plants and flowers. A greenhouse has a glass roof. The sun comes through the roof. The sun keeps the greenhouse warm. Sometimes the walls are also glass. Other times greenhouse walls and roofs are clear plastic instead of glass.

People can control the temperature in a greenhouse. This way, plants can grow all year, even if it's cold outside. When it's not sunny outside, bright lights are turned on over the plants. People or machines water the plants.

There are greenhouses all over the world. Some greenhouses sell plants, vegetables, and food to grocery stores. Other greenhouses sell plants and flowers to people. See if there's a small greenhouse in your town or city. Walk around and look at the plants. Maybe you'll even want to buy one to take home!

Cross out the word that doesn't complete each phrase.

1. A greenhouse roof is made of . . .

      glass   **metal**   **plastic**

2. Greenhouse walls are made of . . .

      plastic   **glass**   **water**

3. . . . grow in greenhouses

      machines   **plants**   **vegetables**

4. Plants in greenhouses get . . .

      light   **water**   **cold**

5. . . . water plants

      people   **machines**   **animals**

Growing Up

Match the young plants with the grown plants.

Lots of Oranges

Welcome to
ORANGE
Population 3,330

Read this chart about five cities named Orange.

City	State	Population (number of people)	Weather	Attractions
Orange	California	138,000	warm all year	small zoo and wildlife sanctuary
Orange	New York	1,800	four seasons	Lamoka Lake
Orange	Texas	19,000	warm all year	art museum, botanical gardens, and nature center
Orange City	Florida	6,600	warm all year	large park
Orange	Ohio	3,300	four seasons	golf course

Use the chart to answer the questions.

1. Which city has the fewest people? _____

2. Which city has the most people? _____

3. Which city has an art museum? _____

4. Which city is Lamoka Lake in? _____

5. Which city has a large park? _____

Knock-Knock

Circle the correct word in parentheses to complete each sentence.

1. A (boy / girl) is telling a joke.

2. The girl says "banana" (three / four) times.

3. The boy asks "Who's there?" (three / four) times.

4. In the last part of the joke "Orange you" sounds like
(Aren't you / Be you).

Nine-Step Orange Juice

It's easy to make orange juice. Start with a ripe orange. Leave the peel on. Give it a squeeze to make it soft. Cut the orange in half. Make sure you have an adult help you cut. Remove the seeds. Then cut around each orange half, just inside the peel. Throw away the peels. Next, hold one of the orange halves tightly. Squeeze it over a bowl. Keep squeezing until all of the juice is in the bowl. Repeat with the other half. Pour the orange juice through a strainer. Throw away the pulp. Pour the orange juice in a glass. Drink the orange juice!

Number the steps in the correct order.

Ollie the Orange-Eating Monkey

Ollie was a little monkey. His parents taught him a lot about living in the jungle. They taught him what to eat. They taught him how to clean himself. They taught him how to swing from vines.

Ollie was good at learning. He was one of the cleanest monkeys in the jungle. He was one of the fastest vine-swingers, too. But Ollie was not good at eating monkey food. Monkeys eat fruit, leaves, seeds, nuts, and insects. They even eat flowers and spiders! But Ollie hated spiders. He hated insects. He liked smelling flowers, but he hated eating them. He didn't like leaves and nuts, either. The only thing Ollie liked to eat was oranges!

Ollie ate oranges for breakfast, lunch, and dinner. His friends told him he was turning orange! They thought it was funny. His parents were worried. They didn't think he was getting enough vitamins. Then his mother started making orange shakes. She would sneak in leaves, seeds, flowers, and insects. Ollie didn't know it, and he loved the orange shakes!

For each pair, circle the picture that is true about Ollie.

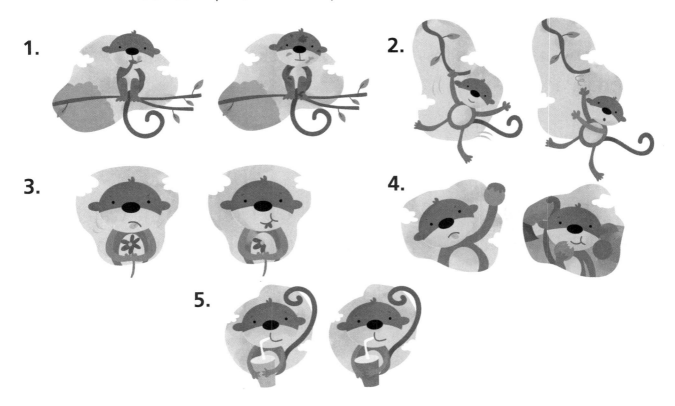

Yellowstone

Yellowstone National Park is the oldest national park in the world. The park spreads into three different states: Wyoming, Idaho, and Montana. It is huge!

Yellowstone is famous for its geysers. A geyser shoots hot water into the air. The water comes from under the ground. Old Faithful is the most famous geyser in Yellowstone. It's called Old Faithful because it erupts or shoots water regularly. It erupts about every hour and a half. The water usually shoots about 150 feet high. That's like 30 people standing on top of each other!

There are many lakes, canyons, rivers, and mountains in Yellowstone. There is also a lot of wildlife. There are hundreds of mammals, birds, fish, and reptiles. Some of the animals are: wolves, bears, moose, bighorn sheep, mountain lions, mountain goats, and deer.

Answer the questions about the reading. Circle the letter of the answer.

1. How many states is Yellowstone National Park in?

a. three
b. five

2. What is Old Faithful?

a. a volcano
b. a geyser

3. What does **regularly** in paragraph 2 mean?

a. repeatedly, at about the same time
b. never

4. How high does the water go up when Old Faithful erupts?

a. 30 feet
b. 150 feet

Bertha the Bighorn Sheep

Bertha is a beautiful gray and white bighorn sheep. The big horns she has on her head are curved a little bit. Her brother Bruce has very big horns that curve a lot. Bertha and Bruce live in Yellowstone National Park. They have a very nice life there. They are wild, but since they live in Yellowstone, people cannot hunt them.

Bertha and Bruce are fully grown sheep. Bertha weighs 200 pounds and Bruce weighs 300 pounds. On a typical day, they walk around the park and graze. That means they eat plants and grass. They also climb the mountains in Yellowstone. They climb high to get away from coyotes and cougars.

One thing they don't like is having their picture taken. Tourists are always trying to take their picture.

Which sheep? Place a check in the correct column. Sometimes the answer is both.

	Bertha	Bruce
1. Has horns that curve a lot		
2. Eats grass		
3. Weighs about 200 pounds		
4. Weighs about 300 pounds		
5. Can climb mountains		

Yellow Sun?

The sun is a star. It is at the center of our solar system. Eight planets orbit the sun. Up close the sun is white, but from earth, it looks yellow. When the sun is lower in the sky, such as at sunset, it looks red, pink, or orange. During the day, the sun looks yellow. But the whole time, day and night, the sun is really white.

From earth, the sun often looks like a giant ball. Close up it is a perfect sphere, too. The sun is enormous. If you put 100 earths side by side, the sun would still be wider!

The heat and light the sun provides is very important to life on earth. Plants and animals would not be able to live without it. Every living thing on earth depends on this white ball of fire!

Match each word to its synonym, or word that means the same thing.

orbit   ball

enormous   needs

sphere   gives

provides   very big

depends on   go around

102

Letter Shuffle

Read the directions and look at the pictures. Write the words.
The first one is done for you.

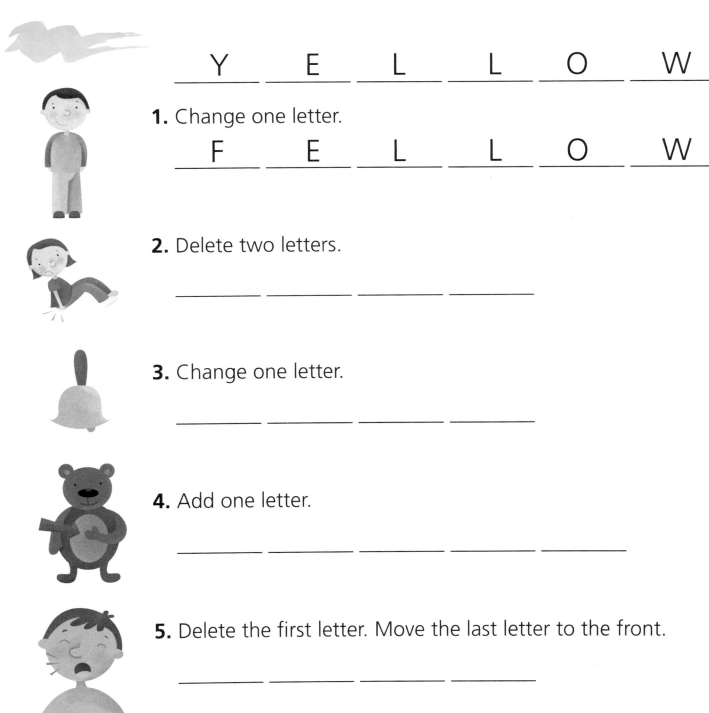

Y   E   L   L   O   W

1. Change one letter.

F   E   L   L   O   W

2. Delete two letters.

____ ____ ____ ____

3. Change one letter.

____ ____ ____ ____

4. Add one letter.

____ ____ ____ ____

5. Delete the first letter. Move the last letter to the front.

____ ____ ____ ____

The Purple Rose

The Purple Rose sounds like a beautiful and unusual flower. It is actually the name of a theater. The theater is in the state of Michigan. It opened in 1991.

The Purple Rose is a theater for actors and writers. The theater offers many classes to learn about acting. In one class, actors can learn how to move their bodies on stage. They also learn about how to use their voices. There is even a class called Kid Purple. It is for children 8 to 12 years old. Students write a short play, design the set, and act in it!

Four plays are performed at the Purple Rose every year. Tickets to these plays are not too expensive. The owners of the Purple Rose think everyone should be able to enjoy a play!

Write **true** or **false** after each statement about the reading.

1. The purple rose is a flower that grows in Michigan.

_____

2. The theater has classes. _____

3. Kids cannot take classes at the theater. _____

4. The theater opened in 1981. _____

5. The tickets are not very expensive at the theater.

_____

Play Time

Use the pictures to write a story about what happened in the school play.

_____

_____

_____

_____

_____

_____

_____

_____

_____

_____

_____

A Plate of Purple

There are a lot of foods that are green. For example, lettuce, beans, peas, and limes are green. But have you ever thought about all the foods that are purple? Here are a few.

Eggplant: Eggplant is a fruit. The outside of it is deep purple. It is shaped like a pear, but it's much larger. It is usually cooked.

Grapes: These are yummy eaten fresh. They are also used to make grape juice.

Plum: A plum is a small fruit that grows on trees. It is shaped like a peach, but it is smaller.

Purple onion: A purple onion is like a white or yellow onion, but it has white and purple rings. Sometimes it is called a red onion.

Blackberries: Blackberries aren't really black. They are a very dark purple fruit. They taste and look a lot like raspberries.

Purple potato: These potatoes are even purple on the inside.

Label the purple foods.

1. _____   2. _____

3. _____   4. _____

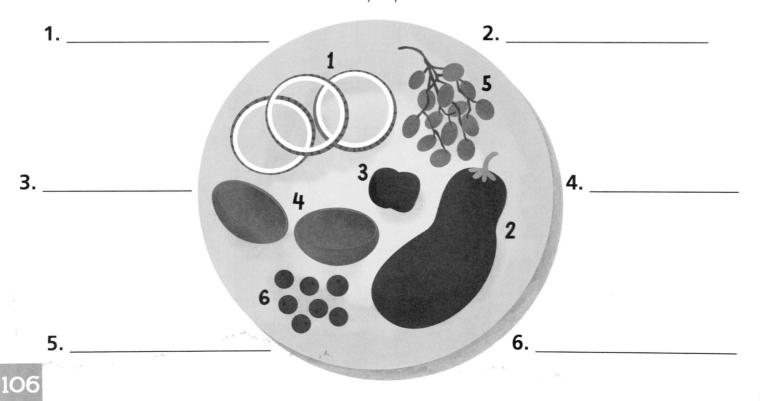

5. _____   6. _____

Paul's Pyramid

Morning, noon, and night, all Paul Plimpton wanted to eat was peanut butter and bread. His mom started to worry. "To be healthy, you have to eat foods from every area of the food pyramid," she said. She showed him a pyramid with five areas: fruits, vegetables, milk, grains, and meat. She explained that Paul would have to eat foods from each group every day for a week.

At first, Paul was angry. He wanted peanut butter! But soon, he became too hungry to refuse the new foods his mom offered. He tried fresh strawberries, ripe bananas, and juicy grapes. He ate crisp green beans and delicious corn on the cob. He drank cold milk. He ate whole wheat bread and oatmeal. He tried baked chicken and pork chops. Every day brought a new taste!

After seven days, Paul's mom was proud. "You have eaten a balanced diet. If you'd like, I will make you a peanut butter sandwich." "No thanks," said Paul. "I want to try something new."

Write the name of each food from the story in the correct place in the food pyramid.

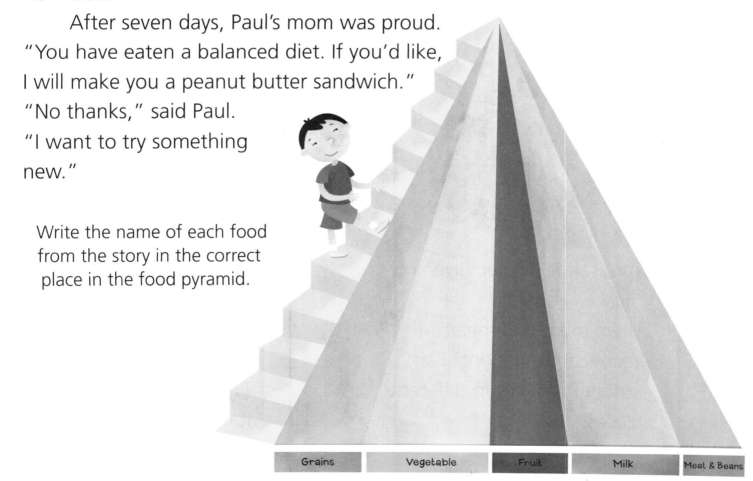

Grains   Vegetable   Fruit   Milk   Meat & Beans

Brown Bears

Look at the pictures. Write **M** for main idea. Write **S** for supporting detail.

1.

_____ Brown bears eat fish.

_____ Brown bears eat berries.

_____ Brown bears eat many things.

2.

_____ Brown bears are huge.

_____ They are nine feet tall.

_____ They weigh 300–1,500 pounds.

3.

_____ Thousands of them live in Alaska.

_____ There are brown bears in Yellowstone National Park.

_____ Brown bears live in different places.

4.

_____ They sleep through most of the winter.

_____ Brown bears sleep a lot.

_____ They sleep during the day and are awake at night.

Brownie Likes Brownies

Brownie is a brown bear. She lives in Alaska. She got her name because she likes to eat brownies! She goes to campsites at night when people are sleeping. She gets into their tents and coolers and eats their food. Her favorite "people food" is brownies!

Her family tells her that she shouldn't go to campsites. They tell her it is dangerous. People are afraid of bears and might think she's attacking them. Those people might hurt her. Her family doesn't think people will understand that Brownie just wants brownies.

They tell Brownie she needs to eat fish and berries. She tries them and she likes them, but they aren't as good as brownies. One day, she finds a store that has been abandoned. No people are in it. There are boxes and boxes of brownie mix. She takes the brownie mix. She learns how to make brownies over a campfire. She adds berries to them and shares them with her family! She never needs to go to a campsite again.

Answer the questions about the story.

1. Where does Brownie live? _____

2. What does Brownie like to eat? _____

3. What does Brownie's family want her to eat?

_____

4. What does Brownie find in the abandoned store?

_____

5. What does she put in her brownies?_____

Beatrice and the Brownout

It was a very hot day in the city. Beatrice was sitting at her desk doing homework. The air conditioner was on. The radio was on. The computer was on. In the other room, she could hear the TV. Suddenly, the lights went dim. What was going on?

"We're having a brownout," said Beatrice's dad. "When people all over the city use too much electricity, there is not enough to go around."

"What should we do?" asked Beatrice.

"We should turn off all of the things that use electricity," said her dad. "That way, we can conserve, or save, electricity. Otherwise, we might have a blackout. If we have a blackout, there will be no electricity at all!"

Beatrice turned off her radio. Her dad turned off the TV, the computer, and the air conditioner.

"I have an idea!" said Beatrice. "Can I turn off my bedroom light and do my homework by candlelight?"

Beatrice's dad thought that was a nice way to help save electricity. In a brownout, it's important to turn off things that use electricity.

Circle the items below that use electricity.

TV	ball	radio
videogame	computer	doll
lamp	bicycle	air conditioner

Brown-Bag It!

Write three words in each bag. The first one has been done for you.

brown
_____

_____

_____

Words that start with br

_____

_____

_____

Brown animals

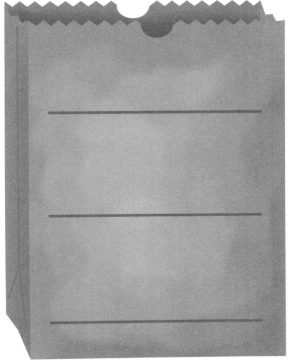

_____

_____

_____

Words that rhyme with brown

_____

_____

_____

Brown foods

Black Facts

Blackout: A blackout is when the power goes out entirely in a city.

Blackberry: A blackberry is a fruit. It is also the name of an electronic device. The device is small and you can send e-mail from it.

Blackboard: This is a board in classrooms. You write on it with chalk. In the past, the boards were always black.

Black-eyed pea: A black-eyed pea is actually a bean. It is very small, like a pea. It is a light color with a black dot, like an eye.

Black belt: In karate, different levels have different-colored belts. The black belt is the highest level in karate.

Black diamond: In downhill skiing, a black diamond is a difficult trail.

Use the facts you learned to fill in the blanks.

1. John is the best in his karate class. He has a _____.

2. Paul can ski very well. He can even ski down a _____.

3. Susana left her _____ at work. Now she can't e-mail on the train.

4. Todd said he couldn't do his homework last night because there was a _____.

5. Lydia's mom had a _____ in her school. Her teacher wrote with chalk. Lydia has a whiteboard in her class. Her teacher writes on it with a marker.

How Bluebirds Became Crows

A compound word is made by joining two shorter words.
Underline the compound words in the story.

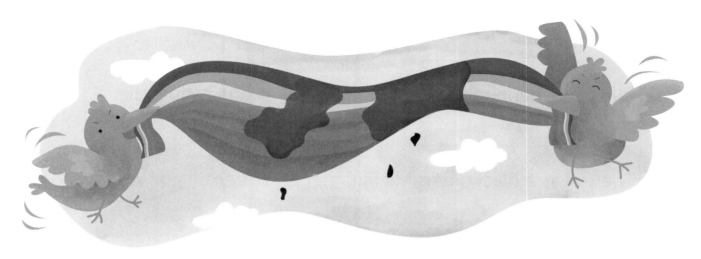

Once upon a time, there were twin baby bluebirds. Their names were Birdie and Blue. They lived in the country, near an old farmhouse. Every morning, it rained. Every afternoon, a beautiful rainbow appeared.

One day, the bluebirds' mother said, "I put that rainbow in the sky just for you!"

When they heard this, the twins began to argue. Blue said, "That's my rainbow." Birdie said, "No, it's mine." They fought for a long time. Then they each flew up and grabbed an end of the rainbow. They pulled and pulled. Each one tried to take it home. The rainbow twisted and turned. All of the colors mixed together. It became black. It turned the bluebirds' beautiful feathers black. The birds became crows.

All About Blackouts

Write **fact** or **opinion** after each statement.

1. A blackout would be the worst thing that could happen in this city.

_____

2. Blackouts happen when there isn't any electricity in a place.

_____

3. There was a blackout in Michigan in 2007 because of a snowstorm.

_____

4. Michigan wouldn't be a good place to live.

_____

5. More than 1 million people lost electricity in Florida in 2005.

_____

6. Florida isn't a good place to visit.

_____

Common Compounds

Match the words to make two compound words. Then use the words to label the pictures. An example is done for you.

1. ___notebook___

   ___bookshelf___

2. _____

   _____

sun	book	shelf
home	light	house
black	work	side
note	out	out

3. _____

   _____

4. _____

   _____

Black-and-White Photography

Ansel Adams was an American photographer who lived from 1902 to 1984. He was most famous for his photos of the western United States. They included landscapes of mountains, forests, and rivers.

Ansel Adams took photographs in a style called straight photography. He took photos that showed things in a very simple way. In 1932, he became part of a group of photographers that helped make the style popular.

In 1940, Ansel Adams helped create the Department of Photography at the Museum of Modern Art in New York City. Six years later, he started the United States' first photography department at the California School of Fine Arts. He also wrote several books on photography.

Answer the questions about the reading.

1. How old was Ansel Adams when he died? _____

2. What did Ansel Adams take pictures of? _____

3. What photography style did Ansel Adams use? _____

4. Where is the Museum of Modern Art? _____

5. In what year did Ansel Adams start the photography department at the California School of Fine arts? _____

Cool Colors

Follow the directions.

1. A noun is a person, place, or thing. Color the nouns green.

2. A verb is a word that shows action. Color the verbs brown.

3. Adjectives are describing words. Color the adjectives red.

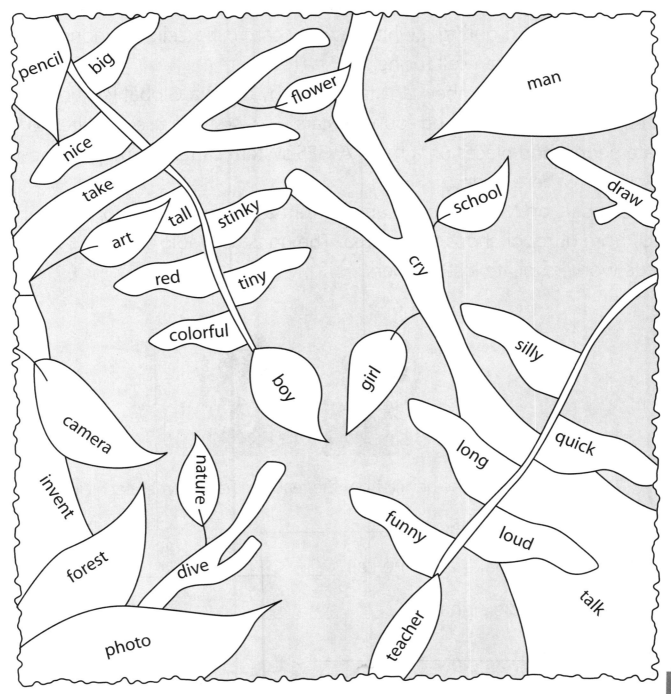

Big Blizzards!

Imagine weather so white that you can't see. That's what happens during a whiteout. Snow and ice make the ground white. Clouds make the sky white. It becomes difficult to tell the ground from the sky. It is easy to lose your sense of direction, especially if snow begins to fall.

Whiteouts are common on Mount Hood in Oregon. They can cause climbers to lose their way on the mountain. One way that climbers can prevent getting lost during a whiteout is by carrying a cellular phone. With a phone, a climber can call for help.

Another way a climber can stay safe is by using a Global Positioning System, or GPS, like the kind found in cars. GPS systems use satellites to locate people and places on a map. A GPS system can use a map to show a lost climber where to go.

Climbers on Mount Hood can also rent a Mountain Locator Unit, or MLU, from outdoor shops in the area. The units use radio signals that help rescue workers locate lost climbers.

Write the name of the device from the reading that matches each clue.

1. Uses satellite signals _____

2. Lets climbers make a phone call _____

3. Sends out radio signals _____

4. Uses a map _____

White Tigers

White tigers are very rare. In fact, there are only a few of these special tigers in the world. Today, about 100 white tigers are living in zoos. All of these are related to a famous white cub tiger named Mohan. Mohan was captured in India in 1951.

White tigers have black or chocolate-brown stripes and blue eyes. This is unique because other tigers have yellow eyes. In many other ways, white tigers are just like other tigers. In fact, an orange tiger can give birth to a white tiger. This is like a brown-haired human having a red-haired baby. It's not common, but it can happen!

White tigers do not have the coloring that helps other tigers blend into the jungles where they live. This means that the white tiger is easier to spot. However, the white tiger is also unusually large. Its bigger size may help it survive in the wild.

Write **true** or **false** after each statement about the reading.

1. Mohan was captured in Africa in 1951. _____

2. White tigers can have black or brown stripes. _____

3. Orange tigers and white tigers are different in every way.

_____

4. All tigers have blue eyes. _____

5. An orange mother tiger can have a white tiger cub.

_____

The White House

How Many of Each Does the White House Have?

Dining rooms	3	Bedrooms	11
Doors	412	Bathrooms	35
Swimming pools	1	Kitchens	3
Fireplaces	28	Libraries	1
Movie theaters	1	Staircases	8
Elevators	3	Windows	147

Compare. Write **<** , **>**, or **=**. The first one is done for you.

> < means "less than"
> > means "more than"
> = means "equal to"

1. swimming pools ____**=**____ libraries

2. doors _____ windows

3. bathrooms _____ bedrooms

4. staircases _____ elevators

5. movie theaters _____ fireplaces

6. dining rooms _____ kitchens

Farah's Field Trip

Farah's class went on a field trip to the White House. The White House is where the president of the United States lives and works. It is in Washington, D.C. Farah was excited to see the White House.

First, they went to the visitor's center. It was like a small museum. There was a lot of information about the history of the White House. They even watched a short video. Farah went to the gift area. She bought a large coin with the White House on one side of it.

Next, the class went on a tour of the White House. They couldn't see all of the rooms, but they saw many. Farah's favorite was the Map Room. There was a map in it that was more than 250 years old! She also liked the Red Room. Even the walls were red!

Farah and her class got back on the bus. Farah and her friend Jack both wanted to get one last look at the White House. They flipped Farah's new coin to decide who got the window seat. Farah won! It was a great day.

Number the events in the correct order.

_____ Farah and her class went back to the bus.

_____ She watched a video about the White House.

_____ She flipped a coin with Jack.

_____ Farah went to Washington, D.C., with her class.

_____ She saw an old map in the Map Room.

Circle Stories

The Frisbee is a disk, or a flat plate shaped like a circle. Frisbee is actually the brand name of a toy. This toy is really called a flying disk, but most people just call it a Frisbee. The first flying disks were used as weapons. About 50 years ago, they became toys. Some people say that the toy got its name from the Frisbee pie company. The company sold pies in tin dishes. College students bought the pies and ate them. Then they would toss the pie tins back and forth for fun. Later, the plastic flying disk was invented to do the same thing.

Different companies called the flying disk by different names. Names included the Pluto Platter, the Whirlo-Way, and the Wham-O. Later, one company called it the Frisbee. Since then, everyone has called it the Frisbee!

Use what you learned from the reading to fill in the blanks.

1. Flying disks were first used as _____.

2. Frisbee was the name of a _____ company.

3. The Frisbee was invented when college students threw pie

_____ for fun.

4. Frisbees are made of _____.

5. Frisbees became toys about _____ years ago.

Circle It!

Remember, a noun is a person, place, or thing. A verb is an action word. Fill in the Venn diagram using words from the word bank. Put nouns in the left circle, verbs in the right circle, and words that can be both in the area where the circles overlap.

go	disk	circle
invention	ask	bicycle
pie	watch	sell

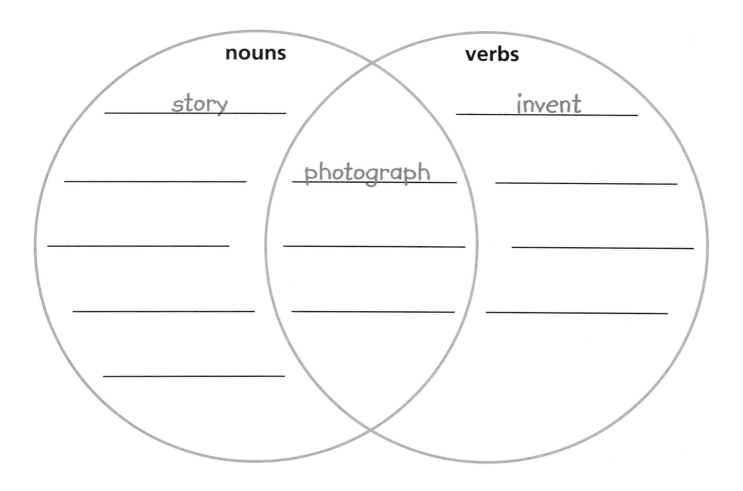

nouns   **verbs**

story   invent

photograph

Share a Square

Square dancing is a kind of dance. Eight people form a square in this dance. Two people are paired together on each side of the square. Music is played. A caller tells the dancers what to do. The dancers know the different dance moves, but they don't know which one the caller is going to tell them to do. They have to follow directions while they dance.

Square Dancing Moves

Swing your partner round and round: This means join arms with your partner and swing around.

Promenade: This means "walk." Sometimes the dancers will walk in a circle with their partners.

Follow your neighbor: This is when all eight dancers walk in a circle. They follow the person in front of them.

Do-si-do: This is when the partners are back-to-back. They make a circle around each other with their backs to each other.

Go home: This is when dancers go to their starting positions to make a square.

Write **true** or **false** after each sentence about square dancing.

1. In square dancing, dancers start in a square. _____

2. A caller dances in the middle of the square. _____

3. Sometimes the dancers form a circle. _____

4. Promenade means "swing around." _____

Times Square

Times Square is a famous area in New York City. It is made up of several blocks around the intersection of Broadway and 42nd Streets. This area is full of restaurants, stores, and theaters that show musicals and plays. Times Square is named after the *New York Times*, the city's largest newspaper, which used to have offices in the area.

Times Square is perhaps best known for its New Year's Eve celebrations. Thousands of people gather there every year on December 31. They wait in the cold for hours to witness a giant crystal ball being lowered from a crane. Ten seconds before midnight, the crowd begins to count backward. The ball drops slowly. When the clock strikes midnight, the ball lights up. Confetti showers down from the buildings overhead. People cheer and blow noisemakers. Friends and families hug and kiss. Strangers wish each other a happy new year. This huge celebration is shown on television.

Match each word to its meaning.

intersection	party
witness	maybe
shower	fall
celebration	a place where two roads meet
perhaps	see

A Terrible Triangle?

The Bermuda Triangle is an area of the Atlantic Ocean between Florida, Puerto Rico, and Bermuda. Some people believe it is a mysterious place. In 1918, the U.S.S. *Cyclops* disappeared from the area. No trace of the huge ship or its 309 passengers was ever found. In 1945, five U.S. airplanes vanished in the area. The seaplane sent to search for them also disappeared. Many other boats, ships, and airplanes have mysteriously gone missing from the area.

Many scientists think the Bermuda Triangle is a misunderstood place. They think that most disappearances from the Bermuda Triangle can be easily explained. The area has strong waves and high winds. It also has hurricanes. Yet hundreds  of boats and airplanes pass safely through the Bermuda Triangle every day. There is no proof that the area has more accidents than any other part of the ocean.

Answer the questions about the reading. Circle the answer.

1. Where is the Bermuda Triangle?

in Bermuda   in the Atlantic Ocean   on a boat

2. In what year did the U.S.S. *Cyclops* disappear?

1945   1918   2004

3. What might have caused some of the disappearances?

fire   hurricanes   lights

4. Who thinks the Bermuda Triangle is misunderstood?

pilots   Christopher Columbus   scientists

"Tri" It!

Add prefixes to the words in the word bank to make new words.
The first one is done for you.

honest	appear	understood
believable	take	explained
~~known~~	place	agree

_____

un-

_____ __unknown__

mis-

_____ _____

dis-

_____ _____

Stop It!

Use the reading to label the parts of the sign.

The stop sign is the same everywhere in the United States. It is easy to recognize. It is a bright red octagon. An octagon has eight sides. This shape makes the stop sign easy to see—even from far away. But the stop sign didn't always look like this. The stop sign first appeared in Michigan in 1915. The sign was white and the letters STOP were black. In 1924, the stop sign was yellow with black letters. The stop sign changed several more times until 1971, when it changed to what it looks like today. Today, the stop sign is red with white letters. The letters are 10 inches high. The sign is 30 inches wide and 30 inches high. There is a $\frac{3}{4}$-inch white border around the outside of the sign.

The sign is usually put on a post. The bottom of the sign is seven feet from the ground. In the past, it was only three feet from the ground. People decided it was too low and hard to see. Today, a stop sign is hard to miss. But if you miss it, you might get a ticket!

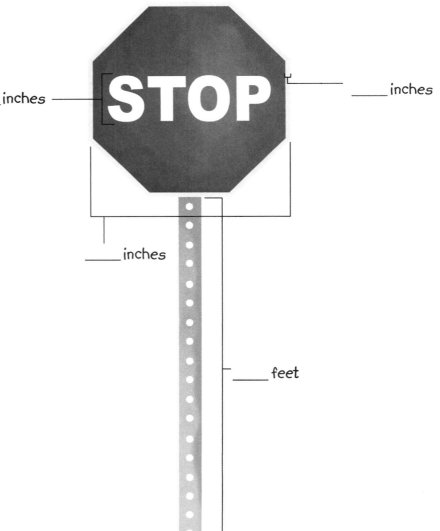

_____ inches

_____ inches

_____ inches

_____ feet

Out of Octagons

Make words using any of these letters. Try to write at least five words in each octagon.

OCTAGONS

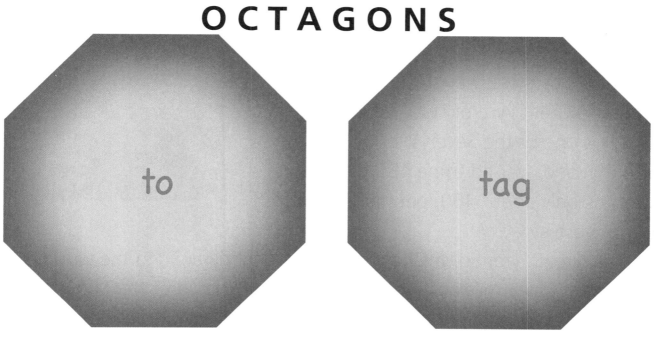

to

Two-Letter Words

tag

Three-Letter Words

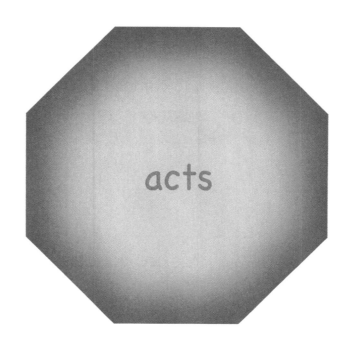

acts

Four-Letter Words

Perfect Pyramids

A pyramid has four sides. Each side is shaped like a triangle. Long ago, people made pyramid-shaped buildings. Many of these pyramids are still standing today.

There are more than 100 pyramids in Egypt. The Great Pyramid of Giza is one of them. It is one of the Seven Wonders of the Ancient World. It used to be 485 feet high. Today it is only about 450 feet high because the top wore away.

The Great Pyramid of Cholula is the largest pyramid in the world. It is in Mexico. It has 5 miles of tunnels inside. The Pyramid of the Sun is also in Mexico. It's smaller than the Great Pyramid of Cholula. It is about 216 feet high. It has steps going up the sides that tourists can climb.

The Pyramid of Cestius is in Italy. It has paintings on the walls inside. Many of the paintings eroded, but people can still see some of them. This pyramid is 120 feet high.

Use the reading to complete the chart.

Pyramid	Country	Fact
Great pyramid of Giza		
		has five miles of tunnels
	Mexico	has steps going up the sides
		has paintings on the wall

Tim's Trip

Complete the postcard. Use the words from the word bank.

huge	Mexico	Spanish	Sun
sunny	outside	inside	

Dear Luke,
   Greetings from _____! I'm having a great time. Today we went to the Pyramid of the _____ and the Pyramid of the Moon. The Pyramid of the Sun is _____. It's 216 feet high. It was built over a cave! We couldn't go _____ the cave. People can walk up the steps on the _____ of the

pyramid. My sister and I walked all the way to the top. We counted the steps. There are 365 of them! There was a great view at the top.
   Tomorrow we're going to the playa. That means "beach" in _____. I hope it's _____. So far, it's been very hot here. I wish you were here.
   Your friend,
   Tim

Sunny-Side Up

Destiny and her dad are making eggs sunny-side up.
Number the pictures in the correct order.

Sunny's Sisters

Sunny Meyers was born on a sunny day, so her parents named her Sunny. When Sunny was five, her parents had a baby girl. Sunny's new sister was born on a snowy day. She wanted to name the baby Snowy.

Her father said, "It can be sunny all year, but it only snows in the winter. Snowy would not be a good name in the spring, summer, and fall." So, they named the baby Lucy.

When Sunny was seven, her parents adopted a baby girl. They brought her home on a very windy day. Sunny thought of a great name. She said, "Let's name her Windy!"

At first, her parents did not like the idea. But they thought about it for a little while. Then her dad said, "How about Wendy? It sounds like Windy." Sunny liked the compromise. She also liked her new sister. She was very happy.

Answer the questions about the story. Circle the answer.

1. Who is the main character of the story?

Lucy   Sunny   Wendy

2. What is the setting of the story?

a house   a spaceship   a park

3. What is the tone of the story?

serious   sad   funny

Rainy Rain Forests

Rain forests are found where the weather is warm. These thick forests get a lot of rain. Some areas get about 80 inches of rainfall every year. There are many tall trees in a rain forest. Some trees can be 165 feet tall!

Many animals live in the tall trees of the rain forests. Frogs, lizards, snakes, and sloths make the branches home. Some animals jump between the trees. Others, like the flying lemur, can glide from branch to branch. Porcupines, opossums, and monkeys can hang from their tails high above the forest floor. Colorful birds nest there, too. Butterflies, bees, ants, moths, and spiders also inhabit the wet woods. In fact, half of all the world's plants and animals live in the rain forest!

Place a check next to the things that can be found in a rain forest.

_____ lizards

_____ whales

_____ a lot of sun

_____ a lot of rain

_____ plants

_____ birds

_____ beds

_____ trees

Rain, Rain, Go Away

One rainy day, Jeremy tried to hold his umbrella while he rode his bike to school. It was impossible! He kept losing his balance. He got soaking wet. This gave him an idea. He cut the handle off his umbrella. He taped the umbrella to the top of his hat. He put the hat on his head. The umbrella was too heavy. It kept falling off his hat.

Jeremy decided to change his invention. He bought a smaller umbrella. He bought a bigger hat. He cut the handle off the smaller umbrella and taped it to his hat. It worked!

He went everywhere with his new invention. He called it the Umbrehat. He rode his bike with it on and he didn't get wet! He loved wearing his Umbrehat so much that he wanted rain to fall every day!

Read the three endings. Place a check next to the ending that makes the most sense.

_____ After Jeremy made his invention, it never rained again.

_____ All of Jeremy's friends wanted an Umbrehat.

_____ Jeremy threw his hat in the garbage.

Cloud Forest Fact or Fiction

Nonfiction books tell facts. Fiction books contain made-up stories. Read each sentence below. Write **N** if the sentence belongs in a nonfiction book. Write **F** if it belongs in a fiction book.

1. _____ Cloud forests are similar to rain forests, but they don't get as much rain. They are very cloudy, though.

2. _____ I was walking through a cloud forest, and I saw a big, hairy monster. It had four arms and three legs. I hid behind a large tree.

3. _____ Cloud forests have a lot of moss in them. The moss grows on the forest floor. It also grows on the tree trunks and branches.

4. _____ Cloud forests are usually near mountains.

5. _____ Once upon a time, a jaguar lived in a cloud forest. He was very hungry. He said to his mother, "I'm going to go look for food on the forest floor."

6. _____ You can find many beautiful orchids in a cloud forest.

Cool Clouds

Label each cloud with the number of the poem that describes it.

I look in the sky, way up high. I see lots of clouds floating by.

1. One looks like a monkey
and one looks like a moose.
Another looks like a turkey
riding in a caboose.

2. A parachute goes floating by,
And I think that it might be
A very big orangutan
hanging by its knees.

3. Look at that cloud!
It's a little pup.
It's eating an egg,
sunny-side up.

The Facts on Fog

Fog is a mist of tiny water drops. It is a lot like the clouds you see in the sky. The difference is that fog touches the ground. It can appear suddenly and disappear just as fast. It can also last for several days. Fog can be very dangerous. It prevents drivers from seeing the road. It can be hard for a pilot to land a plane if the runway is foggy. Sometimes flights are canceled on foggy days.

Fog Facts

- The foggiest place in the world is in the ocean. It is called Grand Banks. It is near an island in Canada.

- There is a place in California that has more than 200 foggy days a year.

- A fog machine creates fog. It is used in plays to make the stage look foggy.

- Smog is a mixture of smoke and fog. It is a kind of pollution. It can make breathing difficult.

Write **true** or **false** after each statement about fog.

1. Fog is made of water drops. _____

2. Fog is like a cloud that touches the ground. _____

3. It is easy to drive in the fog. _____

4. The foggiest place on earth is California. _____

5. Smog is a mixture of snow and fog. _____

Foggy Friends

Match each kid to his or her shadow.

Samuel's Snow Cones

A snow cone is a cold treat made from tiny bits of ice. The ice is crushed by hand or with a machine. It is usually formed into a ball. It is put in a cup and topped with flavored syrup.

Samuel Bert invented the snow-cone machine in 1920. He sold snow cones at state fairs in Texas for 65 years. Today, people can buy snow cones at sporting events such as baseball games. They can also buy them at fairs, carnivals, and circuses. Many ice-cream trucks sell snow cones.

It is easy to make snow cones at home. First, buy flavored syrup at the store. Pick your favorite! Ask an adult to help you crush some ice by hand or in a blender. Put the ice in a cup. Pour some syrup over the ice. Eat your snow cone with a spoon or straw!

Answer the questions about the reading.

1. What ingredients are in a snow cone?

_____

2. Who invented the snow-cone machine?

_____

3. When did he invent it?_____

4. How can you crush ice?_____

5. Where can you buy snow cones?

_____

_____

Snow Days

Draw an ending to each picture story.

1.

2.

3.

How to Make Wind Chimes

Use words from the word bank to complete the instructions.

tie	hang	fold	paint	cut

Materials:

a small clay pot with a hole in the top
2 very large plastic beads (with holes)
16 large glass or metal beads (with holes)
string
scissors
paint

Instructions:

1. _____ the pot any way you want. Make it colorful! Let it dry.

2. _____ four pieces of string. Make each piece three times as long as the pot.

3. _____ the four strings in half. Put the folded part of the strings through a large bead. Move the bead 1 inch from the top.

4. Put the eight string ends through the hole in the pot. The very large bead will be on top of the pot. This will make a loop with the strings. Put the string inside the pot through the other very large bead. There will be eight strings inside the pot. _____ a knot under the string.

5. _____ one bead on each piece of string. Put them at different levels, but make sure they are all inside the pot. Tie one bead on the bottom of each piece of string. These beads will hang below the pot.

Chime In!

Place the words from the word bank in the correct wind chime.

bead	through	scissors	string
under	instructions	inside	eight

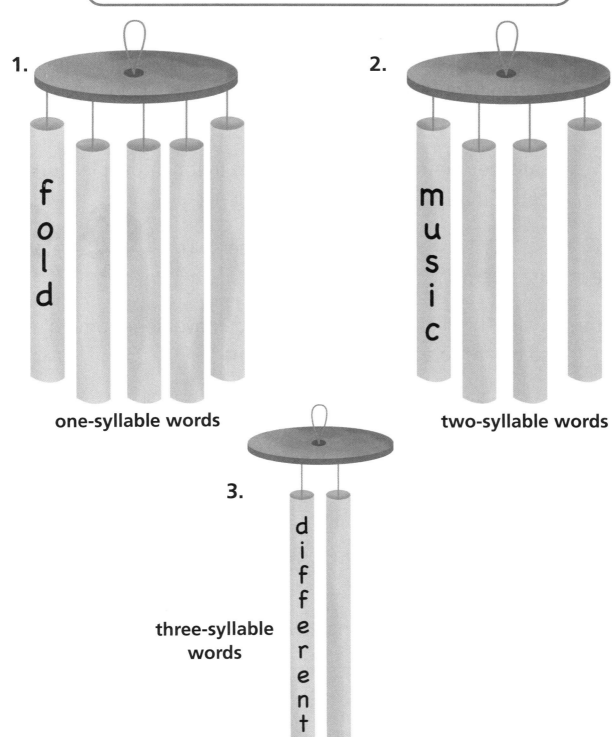

1.

f o l d

one-syllable words

2.

m u s i c

two-syllable words

3.

d i f f e r e n t

three-syllable words

 Face Value

There are many sayings that use the words **head** and **face**. But they don't mean the actual parts of the body. Here are a few popular sayings:

Head of state: This is a ruler or leader of a country.

Heads or tails: These are two sides of a quarter. Heads is the side with George Washington's head on it. Tails is the side with the eagle on it. When people make a decision by flipping a coin, one person chooses heads and one person chooses tails.

Two heads are better than one: This means that two people working together is better than one person working alone.

Face-to-face: This is usually a meeting between two people in the same place.

Face the music: This means to accept that you have done something wrong. It also means to accept the punishment.

Use the sayings you learned to fill in the blanks.

1. John cheated on a test. Now he has to _____.

2. The country's _____ makes important decisions.

3. Lilly and Raul solved the problem together. _____ _____.

4. I don't want to talk on the phone. I want to meet you _____ _____.

5. Let's flip a coin to see who goes first. Do you want _____ _____?

Heads or Tails?

Don and Luisa are neighbors. They play together on Saturdays. Sometimes they climb trees. Sometimes they tell stories. Sometimes they ride their bikes to the park. One Saturday they decide to play a board game. But there is one problem. They both want to go first. They argue about it.

They decide to ask for help. Don's mom says, "Let the youngest person go first." But there is one problem. Their birthdays are on the same day.

Don's dad says, "Luisa should go first because she's a girl." Don doesn't like that idea. Luisa doesn't either.

Don's older brother says, "Flip a coin!" They both think it's a great idea. But there is one problem. They both want heads! They laugh and laugh. Then they decide not to play a game. They ride their bikes to the park instead.

Answer the questions about the story. Circle the answer.

1. What does **play** in paragraph 1 mean?

    act on a stage   do fun things

2. What does **stories** in paragraph 1 mean?

    fictional events   floors in a building

3. What does **their** in paragraph 2 mean?

    Don's and Louisa's   Don and Louisa are

4. What does **heads** in paragraph 4 mean?

    a part of the body   a side of a coin

Eye Can See!

People see with their eyes. Animals see with their eyes, too. Some animals' eyes are like human eyes. Some are very different.

Bats: Bats can see very well, but they are color-blind. They see shapes but not details.

Spiders: Some spiders have two eyes. Others have four or six eyes. Some spiders even have eight eyes! There are spiders that live only in caves. They don't have any eyes. They don't need to see because it's always dark in the caves.

Earthworms: Earthworms do not have any eyes. Instead, cells on the outside of their bodies sense light and help them get around.

Chameleons: Chameleons have two eyes that can move in different directions at the same time. For example, one eye can see something to the right and the other eye can see something different to the left!

Owls: Owls can't move their eyes at all! They must turn their heads to see things in different directions.

Use the reading to complete the chart.

Animal	Quick Fact
	have cells that sense light
	can't move their eyes
	eyes move in different directions
	are color-blind
	some live in caves and don't need eyes

Braille Brainteaser

Braille is the system that blind people use to read and write. It was invented about 100 years ago. In Braille dots are used for letters. Each letter has a different pattern. The dots are raised so that people can feel them with their fingers.

Here are a few letters in Braille. If this were truly Braille, the black dots would be raised, or higher on the page.

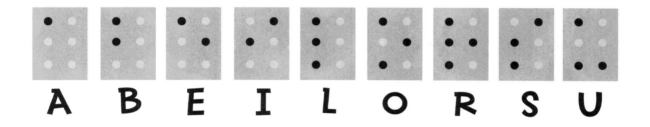

A   B   E   I   L   O   R   S   U

Use the code above to solve the puzzle.

Who invented Braille?

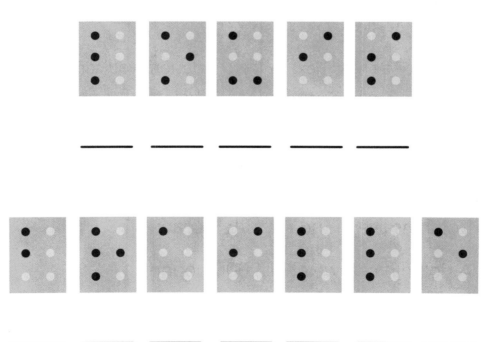

___ ___ ___ ___ ___

___ ___ ___ ___ ___ ___ ___

Those Noses

Bottlenose dolphins are the most common dolphins. They are named for their bottle-shaped snouts. Bottlenose dolphins are light or dark gray. They are white on the bottom. They live in every ocean and sea in the world except the Arctic and Antarctic oceans. They can often be seen jumping from the water into the air. They do this to get oxygen. Like humans, dolphins need to get oxygen from the air to stay alive. They breathe through blowholes on top of their heads.

Dolphin Details

- Adult dolphins are between 6 and 13 feet long.

- They weigh between 330 and 1,430 pounds.

- They usually swim in groups of about ten.

- They eat fish. They have teeth to grab food, but they don't chew it.

- They talk with each other with squeaks and whistles. They also move their bodies to "talk."

Place a check next to the conclusions you can make
based on information from the reading.

1. _____ Dolphins swallow their food whole.

2. _____ Dolphins eat turtles.

3. _____ Dolphins live in the Atlantic Ocean.

4. _____ A dolphin can weigh 12,000 pounds.

5. _____ Dolphins are a kind of whale.

Smelly Stories

Circle the books where you could read about the sense of smell.

The Five Senses

Lakes and Oceans

All About Noses

All About Braille

How Dolphins Talk

Dolphins Don't Smell Well

Animals with No Sense of Smell

Flowers and Their Scents

Hear It! Ear It!

Write words that rhyme with **ear**. Try to write at least three words in each column.

-ear	-ere	-eer
clear	sincere	sneer

Nosey Ears

Leo liked to listen. In fact, he was a little nosey. One day he picked up the phone and listened to his sister's conversation. She said, "Leo, it's not nice to eavesdrop."

But Leo liked eavesdropping. Soon, he was eavesdropping on his teachers, his friends, and his family. It was fun to hear the things people said when they didn't know he was listening!

One night Leo heard his parents whispering in the kitchen. He crouched behind a counter to eavesdrop. He heard them talking about throwing him a surprise party for his birthday. At first, he was thrilled. But suddenly he realized the party would not be a surprise at all. He had spoiled the whole thing! He decided that eavesdropping was not such a good idea.

Answer the questions about the story. Circle the answer.

1. What does **nosey** in paragraph 1 mean?

    a snoop   **a big nose**

2. What does **eavesdrop** in paragraph 1 mean?

    drop something   **listen secretly**

3. What does **crouched** in paragraph 3 mean?

    kneeled down   **jumped up**

4. What does **thrilled** in paragraph 3 mean?

    very happy   **scared**

5. What does **spoiled** in paragraph 3 mean?

    ruined   **fixed**

Tooth Time

It is very important to take care of your teeth. Here are some ways you can keep your teeth healthy.

- Brush your teeth two or three times a day. Brush after every meal, if possible. If not, brush in the morning and at night. Do not brush more than three times a day. This can be bad for your gums.

- Get a new toothbrush every few months. When the bristles start to bend, it's time to get a new toothbrush.

- Use a toothbrush with soft bristles. Medium or hard bristles can hurt your gums.

- Use toothpaste with fluoride in it.

- Floss your teeth once a day.

Circle the picture in each pair that shows the correct way to care for your teeth.

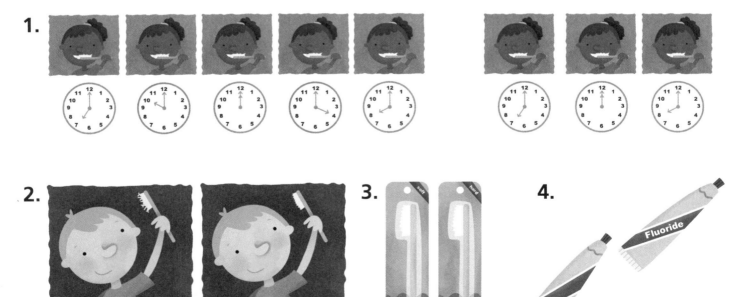

Context Clues

Circle the word that means the same as the underlined word. Use the context, or meaning of the sentence, to help you.

1. Plaque is a clear <u>film</u> that sticks to your teeth.

    movie

    layer   record

2. <u>Bacteria</u> and sugar stick to plaque.

    germs

    candy   toothpaste

3. Bacteria and sugar destroy <u>enamel</u> on your teeth.

    white   the protective layer

                eraser

Types of Ties

A tie is something that you wear around your neck. Usually men wear ties. There are several different kinds of ties.

Necktie: A necktie is a long piece of fabric with a point at the end. It's worn around the neck. It ties in front near the neck.

Bow tie: A bow tie goes around the neck and has a bow in front.

Neckerchief: A neckerchief is a square piece of fabric. It is usually folded in half, and then it is tied around the neck. It can tie in front or in back. Men and women wear neckerchiefs.

Bolo tie: A bolo tie is a long, thin string or rope. It doesn't tie. It hangs from the neck. A fancy pin in front joins the two pieces of string.

Label each tie according to the reading.

1.

_____

2.

_____

3.

_____

4.

_____

Neck-and-Neck

Every year, Pine Elementary School has a race. Anyone can run. This year, everyone thinks that either Mario or Janice will win. They are the fastest kids in the class. The other eight people in the race don't mind if they lose. They want to be in the race anyway. Carly, Dan, Keisha, and Mike just want to run faster than last year. Paul is hoping to come in third. Wendy is in a wheelchair. She's been practicing all year. This is her first race. Ted and Lydia both hope that they're not last.

"On your mark, get set, go!" the announcer says. Everyone takes off.

The crowd cheers, "Go, Mario! Go, Janice! Go, Mike! Go, Wendy! Go, Ted!" They cheer for everyone. Mario and Janice are neck-and-neck for the whole race. They finish in a tie! Ted and Keisha also tie. They both finish last. They're happy to share last place and not be alone.

Match each word or phrase to its meaning.

get set   clap and shout

either   finish at the same time

cheer   get ready

neck-and-neck   very close

tie   one or the other

Armadillos in Armor

Armadillos are unique animals. They live in North America and South America. They live in warm parts of the United States. There are a lot of armadillos in Texas.

An armadillo has a very hard shell. No animal can bite through it. If an animal does attack, the armadillo will run to its burrow or dig a hole with its sharp claws. Armadillos also jump straight up in the air when they're scared. They can jump up to 4 feet!

Most armadillos are about 30 inches long. They have very short legs but they run fast. They also swim. To do this, they fill their stomachs with air. If they don't, they sink! Sometimes they sink on purpose and walk across the bottom of rivers. They can stay under water for six minutes!

Answer the questions about the reading.

1. What continents do armadillos live on?

_____

2. What do armadillos do when they are attacked?

_____

3. How high can armadillos jump?

_____

4. How do armadillos swim?

_____

5. How long can armadillos stay underwater?

_____

Armchair Endings

Circle the correct suffix. Then write the word in the blank.
The first one has been done for you.

1.

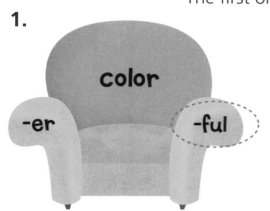

Butterflies are very _____colorful_____.

2.

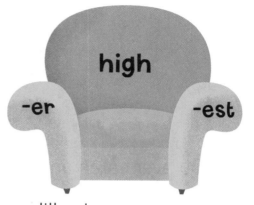

Armadillos jump _____ than kangaroos.

3.

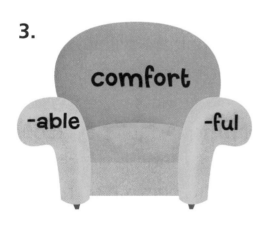

This chair is very _____.

4.

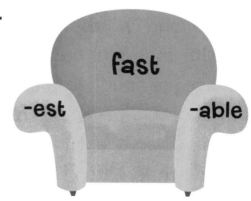

Jorge is the _____ runner in the class.

5.

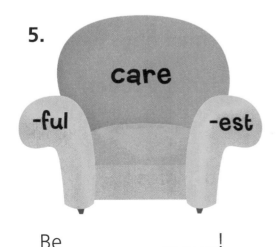

Be _____!

6.

I made some _____ wind chimes in art class.

Edible Elbows?

Have you ever eaten an elbow? What about a bowtie? Elbow macaroni and bowties are two types of pasta. Pasta is a kind of food made from flour. It comes in many different shapes and sizes. Macaroni are hollow tubes that can be bent like elbows. Farfalle are shaped like bowties. Spaghetti are long chords. Noodles are flat strips. Ravioli are pillow-shaped and filled with cheese or meat. Anellini are small rings used in soup.

Pasta means dough in Italian. At pasta factories, flour is mixed with water and other ingredients to form a stiff dough. The dough is rolled out by a machine. Then it is cut into different shapes. The dough is dried until it is hard and brittle. Later, it can be cooked in water to become soft and chewy. Delicious!

Match each noodle to its description.

macaroni	small rings
spaghetti	hollow tubes
ravioli	shaped like pillows
anellini	bowties
farfalle	long chords

Elbow Room

Tabitha had a big family. She lived with her parents, her twin brothers, her older sister, and her baby sister. One night, they were all eating dinner at the table. They bumped elbows many times. Tabitha's father said, "I need more elbow room."

Later, they were sitting on the couch watching TV. Tabitha's mother said, "I need more elbow room."

Tabitha said, "Don't you mean you need more leg room?"

"No," she answered. "Elbow room is a saying. It means you need more space."

At bedtime, Tabitha went into the bedroom she shared with her sisters. She was tired. She wanted to go to sleep but her older sister was talking on her cell phone. Her baby sister was crying.

"I don't need elbow room," said Tabitha. "I need my own room!"

Use what you read in the story to fill in the blanks.

1. Tabitha has twin _____.

2. At dinner, Tabitha's father needs more space for his

_____.

3. Tabitha's mother says that elbow room is a _____.

4. Tabitha shares a room with her _____.

5. Instead of elbow room, Tabitha wants her _____ room.

Handsome Handwriting

Calligraphy is the art of writing. It has been around for thousands of years. Long ago, people in Europe wrote with feathers or sticks cut into pointed shapes. People in Asia used brushes. They wrote down important information.

Many people worked as calligraphers, or writers, before the invention of the typewriter and printing press. Today, a few people still do this as a job. They create designs for book jackets. They handwrite invitations. Some use their handwriting skills to create artwork.

Calligraphy is a popular hobby. A hobby is something people do for fun. You can take calligraphy lessons. There are also books and websites that teach this art. You can use calligraphy to make your own greeting cards, posters, and awards.

Use what you learned from the reading to fill in the blanks.

1. People in _____ used feathers to write.

2. Calligraphy is the art of _____ .

3. A _____ is something people do for fun.

4. You can use _____
to create your own cards and posters.

5. Calligraphy has been around for
_____ of years.

Trevor's Best E-Mail Pal

Trevor loves to e-mail. He sends messages to his friends and family. He even has an "e-mail pal" who lives in India. They exchange messages and pictures about their lives.

One summer, Trevor visits his great-grandmother. She's 87 years old. She tells him stories about her life. He has a wonderful time. When he leaves, she says, "Please write me letters."

"Letters?" Trevor asks. "Great-grandma, we can e-mail each other."

"Oh, Trevor. I don't know how to use a computer!" she says.

Trevor writes a letter to his great-grandmother. A few days later, he gets a letter from her. He decides that letters are not so bad, but next summer, when he visits his great-grandmother again, he will teach her how to use a computer. He knows she'll like getting pictures with e-mails! She will be his best e-mail pal.

Cross out the word or phrase that does **not** complete the sentence about the story.

1. Trevor likes _____.

visiting his great-grandmother

using a computer

writing by hand

2. Trevor writes e-mails to his _____.

family

friends

teacher

3. Trevor's great-grandmother _____.

likes computers

is 87 years old

tells stories

4. Trevor wants to _____.

visit his great-grandmother again

stop using a computer

teach his great-grandmother how to use a computer

Finger Fun

Finger painting is using your fingers to paint. This is popular with little children. They can paint with their fingers before they are old enough to hold a paintbrush. Stores sell special paints for finger painting. It's fun to get messy!

Even adults like to finger paint. Tyler Ramsey is an adult artist. He lives in the state of California. He never uses a paintbrush! He loves to paint with his fingers. He thinks that using his fingers makes his art creative.

Nick Benjamin also finger paints. He lives in London, England. He has been finger painting since 1994.

Jimmy Sudduth is a finger painter from Alabama. He doesn't use paint. He uses materials from the earth, like plants and clay. He finger paints on old doors and boards!

It is easy to finger paint. However, it's not always easy to make a good finger painting. Try it at home and see what kind of art you make.

Write **true** or **false** after each sentence about the reading.

1. You cannot buy finger paint. _____

2. Finger painting is only for kids. _____

3. Tyler Ramsey doesn't use a paintbrush. _____

4. Nick Benjamin lives in Alabama. _____

5. Jimmy Sudduth doesn't paint on paper. _____

Finger Food

1 Fred Franklin loved to eat
2 He liked vegetables
3 He liked meat

4 One day Fred was very sad
5 He had no utensils
6 Things were bad

7 He had no spoon
8 He had no fork
9 He had no knife to cut his pork

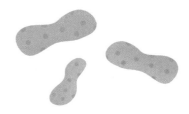

10 Then clever Freddy thought of a plan
11 He'd make finger foods
12 And eat with his hands

Answer the questions about the poem. Circle the letter of the answer.

1. Who is the main character in the poem?

   a. Fred   **b.** finger food

2. What is the tone of the poem?

   a. serious   **b.** funny

3. Who is telling the story?

   a. a narrator   **b.** Fred

4. What does **utensils** in line 5 mean?

   a. things you eat   **b.** things you use to eat

Stomach This

The stomach is an organ. Other organs are the heart, the lungs, and the brain. Stomachs are very important organs. They help people and animals digest food. They make a juice that helps break down food. If there isn't any food in your stomach, the juices move, trying to find food. Sometimes this makes a noise. It's your stomach grumbling. This usually means you need to eat!

Stomach Facts

- Human stomachs are shaped like beans.
- Armadillos inflate their stomachs with air to swim.
- Cattle and sheep have stomachs with four parts.
- Some kinds of worms don't have stomachs.

Follow the directions.

1. Circle the names of four animals.

2. Underline the names of four organs.

3. Draw a wavy line under two things that stomachs do.

4. Put an X above the word that means "fill with air."

5. Draw two lines under the word that means "growling."

Sick to My Stomach

Yesterday, my stomach hurt just a little. When my mom asked me to clean my room, I said, "I can't. I'm sick." My dad told me to do my homework. I said, "I have a stomachache." My grandfather asked me to take out the trash. I said, "Garbage makes me sick to my stomach!"

At dinner, we had peas. I don't like them. My mom told me to eat them anyway. I said, "I can't. I'm really sick." My father asked me to wash the dishes. I said, "My stomach still hurts."

Then my grandfather cut three pieces of chocolate cake. He cut one for my mom, one for my dad, and one for himself. "Where's my cake?" I asked. "Julie," he said, "your stomach hurts."

I went upstairs. I cleaned my room. Then I did my homework. I took out the trash. I ate my cold peas, and I washed the dishes. I went downstairs and said, "I feel better. Can I have a piece of cake?" There was already a big piece of cake for me on the table. My grandfather smiled.

Answer the questions about the story.

1. Who is telling the story?_____

2. How many people are in the story?_____

3. Who asks Julie to clean her room?_____

4. Who asks Julie to do the dishes?_____

5. Do you think Julie was really sick?_____

_____

A Leg to Stand On

There are a lot of sayings that contain the word **leg**. Read about some of them.

Last leg: This is the final part of a race or a journey.

Shake a leg: This doesn't mean to move your leg back and forth. It means to hurry up and do something fast.

Pull your leg: This means you are joking. You might say something that's not true as a joke. Then you tell the person that you are pulling his or her leg.

Break a leg: This sounds terrible, but it really means "good luck." People say this to actors before they go on stage.

Leg it: This means to walk instead of taking a car.

Use the sayings you learned to fill in the blanks.

1. "I'm not going to take the bus today. I'm going to _____ _____."

2. "Come on, Jim. _____! We're going to be late."

3. "I almost didn't finish the _____ of the race."

4. "_____, Paula. I know you will be great!"

5. "I'm not really sick. I just wanted to _____ _____."

Three-Legged Thrill

Martin wanted to be in the three-legged race at the school fair. He asked his friend Jin to be his partner.

She said, "Sure. Who will the third person be?"

Martin said, "No one. There are only two people in a three-legged race. We each put a leg in a sack, so together we have three legs!"

"That sounds fun!" Jin said. "Let's practice."

They practiced for three weeks. They were nervous on the day of the fair. There were ten other pairs in the race. Martin and Jin walked very fast. At one point they fell, but they got back up. The race was 30 yards long. After every 10 yards, they could stop and take a break. They were neck-and-neck with Todd and Bill for most of the race. They pulled ahead in the last leg of the race. They won!

Answer the questions about the story. Circle the answer.

1. What does **fair** in paragraph 1 mean?   carnival   right

2. What does **sack** in paragraph 3 mean?   quit   bag

3. What does **sounds** in paragraph 4 mean?   noises   seems

4. What does **take a break** in paragraph 5 mean? rest   smash

5. What does **ahead** in paragraph 5 mean?

a part of the body   in front

Knee News

Knees are the joints that connect the upper part of the leg to the lower part. You can bend your legs because of your knees. Knees are an important part of the human body.

Many animals have knees, too. It's easy to see elephants' knees. They have a lot of wrinkles on them. Camels kneel on all four of their knees. This is helpful when people ride camels. They can get on the camel while the animal is kneeling. Cattle have knees, but they can't kneel.

Some people say that crickets hear with their knees! That's not quite true. Crickets hear with their ears, but their ears are on their knees. Some people say that flamingos bend their knees backward. This isn't true, either. What look like knees are really ankles! Flamingos' knees are under their feathers. People can't even see their knees.

Write the name of the animal that each sentence describes.

1. They kneel on all fours.   _____

2. Feathers cover their knees.   _____

3. Their knees are wrinkly.   _____

4. They cannot kneel.   _____

5. Their ears are on their knees.   _____

Listen, I'm going to tell you a secret.

Knee Deep

Some letters are silent. Write three words for each letter.
An example has been given for each.

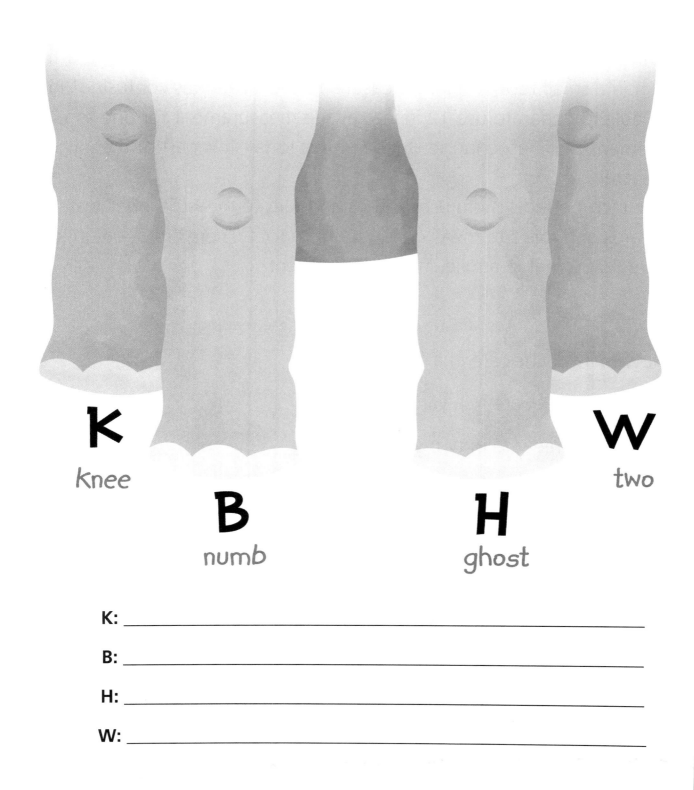

K
knee

B
numb

H
ghost

W
two

K: _____

B: _____

H: _____

W: _____

Foot Facts

A foot is a measurement. It probably got its name because long ago people measured things with their feet. For example, someone could measure the length of a piece of wood by counting the steps from one end to the other. Each step was a foot. But people's feet are different sizes. If the person measuring the wood had a big foot, the wood might measure 8 feet. If the person had a small foot, it might measure 13 feet. This was confusing! In 1305, England began to use 12 inches as the measurement for one foot. That measurement is still used in the United States today. It is part of the inch-pound system.

The inch-pound system uses inches and feet to measure small distances. It uses yards and miles to measure longer distances. There are 3 feet in a yard. There are 5,280 feet in a mile. That's a lot of feet!

Answer the questions about the reading.

1. How many inches are in a foot? _____

2. How many feet are in a yard? _____

3. How many feet are in two yards? _____

4. How many feet are in a mile? _____

5. What country measures with feet? _____

Foot-Long Hot Dogs

Match the words to make compound words.

 foot

 stand

 hand

 stroke

 ear

 glasses

 back

 ball

 eye

 ache

African Waters

Africa is the second largest continent in the world. It is surrounded by the Mediterranean Sea, the Red Sea, the Atlantic Ocean, and the Indian Ocean.

Africa has many rivers and lakes. Lake Victoria is the biggest lake in Africa. It is the third largest lake in the world. It is so big that it is in three different countries! Its deepest part is about 270 feet deep. That's not very deep for a lake. Lake Tanganyika is also in Africa. It's almost 5,000 feet deep!

Africa is home to one of the longest and most famous rivers in the world. The Nile River starts in Egypt and goes through many countries. It breaks into two rivers called the White Nile and the Blue Nile. Many people live in cities near the Nile River. People from all over the world come to see the Nile River.

Follow the directions.

1. Circle the names of two seas.

2. Draw a straight line under the names of two oceans.

3. Put an X above the names of two lakes.

4. Draw a wavy line under the name of a continent.

5. Put a check mark above the name of one long river.

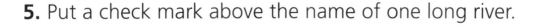

River Rafting

Cam went river rafting on the Nile River. Use the missing pictures to write a story.

Cool Castles

Europe is the second smallest continent in the world. It has about 50 countries. Hundreds of years ago, kings and queens ruled these countries. They lived in castles. Today, there are only a few kings and queens left in Europe. However, many famous castles remain.

Prague Castle is the largest castle in the world. No one lives there anymore. You can take a tour around the gardens. You can even go in some of the rooms.

Another famous castle is Neuschwanstein Castle. It is in Bavaria, Germany. King Ludwig II designed the castle around 1869. Walt Disney later used it as the model for the Sleeping Beauty Castle at Disneyland.

Queen Elizabeth II of England still lives in a castle. In fact, she lives in a few! Her castle in London is called Buckingham Palace. She also has a home in the English countryside. It is called Windsor Castle. When she is in Scotland, the queen stays in Balmoral Castle.

Circle the word in parentheses that correctly completes the sentence.

1. Europe is the second (smallest / biggest / cleanest) continent in the world.

2. There are (about / less than / more than) 50 countries in Europe.

3. (Mr. / King / Queen) Elizabeth II lives in a castle.

4. She has (3 / 30 / 50) castles.

5. Prague Castle is the (smallest / biggest / highest) castle in the world.

An Incorrect Castle

Circle six things that are wrong in the picture.

Only in the Outback

Australia is the only continent that is also a country, a desert, and an island. It is famous for its beautiful scenery and interesting wildlife. It is also known for its outback. This is a large area in the middle of the continent. It is sometimes called the back country.

Most of the outback is very dry and hot. Snakes, lizards, camels, and wild, doglike animals called dingoes live there. Kangaroos and other marsupials also make the outback home. Marsupials are animals that carry their young in pouches.

Very few people live in the outback. Most live on cattle ranches or in tiny towns. These people are far away from hospitals and schools. A service flies doctors to help them. Special schools use computers, phones, and radios to teach students who cannot get to a classroom.

Check **yes** or **no** to complete the chart.

	Yes	No
1. Lots of people live in the outback.		
2. Dingoes live in the outback.		
3. Dolphins live in the outback.		
4. Marsupials carry food in their pouches.		
5. Australia is an island and a country.		

Sort It Out

Read the things from the word bank that are in Australia.
Write them in the correct group.

water lily	koala bear	the outback
Sydney	eucalyptus tree	crocodile
dingo	Lake Mackay	orchid

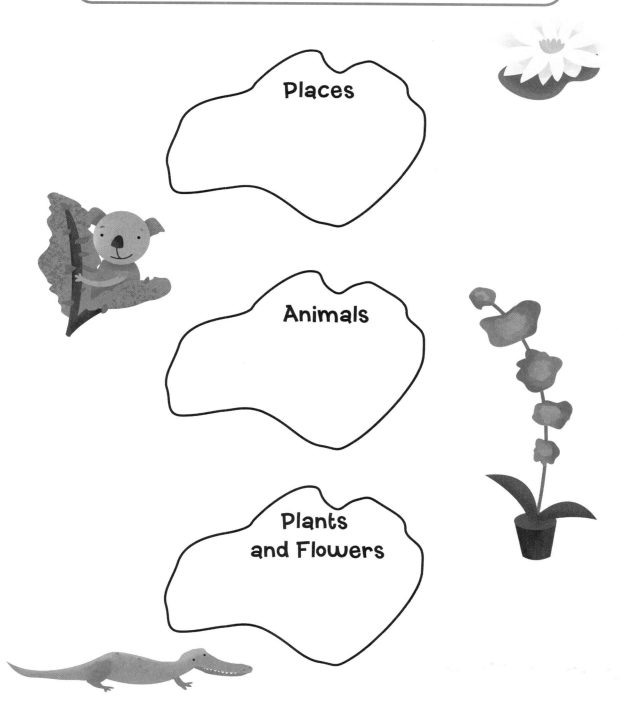

Places

Animals

Plants and Flowers

High in the Sky

Asia is the largest continent in the world. It is the continent with the most people. It is the continent with the most mountains, too. Look at the chart about the five highest mountains in the world. They are all in Asia.

Mountain	Height (about)	Interesting Facts
Makalu	27,824 feet	People think this is the hardest mountain in the world to climb.
K2	28,250 feet	People first climbed this mountain 100 years ago. They didn't get to the top.
Kanchenjunga	28,200 feet	The name **Kanchenjunga** means "the five treasures of the snow." It has five peaks.
Mount Everest	29,000 feet	It is one of the Seven Wonders of the Natural World.
Lhotse	27,900 feet	It is connected to Mount Everest by hills.

Write the names of the Asian mountains.

1. Highest _____

2. Second highest _____

3. Third highest _____

4. Fourth highest _____

5. Fifth highest _____

Mountain Man

I watched a good movie yesterday. I think you would like it. It's called *The Englishman Who Went Up a Hill and Came Down a Mountain*. It's about a man in England. He's a cartographer. That's someone who makes maps. He goes to a small town for his job. He has to measure the mountain in the town. He measures it, but it's not a mountain. It's 16 feet too short to be a mountain. It's only a hill.

The people in the town aren't happy about this. They take dirt to the top of the mountain to make it higher! They try to keep it a secret, but the cartographer finds out. At first, he thinks they're crazy. Then he helps them.

The movie is over ten years old, but it's still good. You should rent it!

Place a check next to the things that happen in the movie.

1. _____ A cartographer goes to a big city.

2. _____ Townspeople try to make a hill into a mountain.

3. _____ The cartographer helps put dirt on top of the hill.

4. _____ The cartographer gets angry with the townspeople.

5. _____ The cartographer helps the townspeople.

Nature Stories

Have you ever wondered why the sky is blue? Have you ever asked how rainbows are made? Humans have always been curious about nature. The first people to live in North America used stories to explain many of the earth's mysteries. These people, called Native Americans, passed the stories from parent to child.

Native American stories often use animals to tell about important events. For example, one story tells how a little spider created the first fire. Another tells about a baby with the beak of a raven. He broke a toy and created light. A third story says that the Big Dipper is a bear being chased across the sky by hunters.

Some stories tell about the animals themselves. For example, one tells about how the rabbit lost its long tail. Others explain how the raven became black and the chipmunk got the stripes on its back. Today, many of the stories appear in books.

Write **true** or **false** after each statement about the reading.

1. Native Americans were the first to live in North America.

_____

2. Native American stories can be found in books. _____

3. One story tells about how a rabbit created fire. _____

4. Many stories are about animals. _____

5. One story tells about the Little Dipper. _____

Bluebird and the Coyote

There once was a little bird. It had brown feathers. There was also a coyote. It also had brown fur. They lived by a bright blue lake.

The bird loved the color of the lake. It went in the water every day for four days. It sang this song every day: "Water, water, can you make me as blue as this lake?" On the fourth day, the bird came out of the lake without feathers. On the fifth day, the bird went in the water again. It sang the song. When it came out of the lake, it had bright blue feathers!

The coyote saw the bird's blue feathers. It wanted to have blue fur. The coyote asked, "How did you turn blue?" The bird told the coyote what happened. The coyote went in the water for four days and sang the song. On the fourth day, the coyote came out of the lake without fur. On the fifth day, it came out of the lake with bright blue fur.

The coyote loved to brag. He ran around the lake saying, "I'm blue! I'm the prettiest animal in the world!" The coyote was so busy bragging that it didn't see a big rock. It tripped over the rock and fell in some brown dirt. Its fur turned brown again. To this day, coyotes are as brown as mud.

Answer the questions about the story.

1. Who are the main characters? _____

2. What is the setting? _____

3. What does this story explain? _____

4. What is the lesson? _____

5. How do you think the coyote felt at the end? _____

Music Makers

Many kinds of music are popular in South America. People like cumbia, tango, rock, and pop, and a lot of other kinds of music. There are many kinds of musical instruments in South American music. Here are a few you might not know.

Cajón: A cajón (say kah-HOHN) is a drum. It looks like a box. A person sits on top of it and hits the sides to make music.

Charango: A charango is a small string instrument. It is similar to a guitar. In the past, it was made from an armadillo shell. Today, it is usually wooden.

Maracas: These are shakers. They have handles and balls at the ends. The balls contain seeds or other items that make noise.

Ocarina: An ocarina is a small flute. It is oval and the size of a small potato. It has a hole for your mouth and small holes on top for your fingers.

Panpipes: Panpipes have ten or more pipes hooked together. It can also be called a zampoña (say zahm-POH-nyah) or a pan flute.

Label the instruments.

1. _____   2. _____   3. _____

4. _____   5. _____

Before or After?

Use the suffixes and prefixes to make new words. The first one has been done for you.

over–	1. _over_ look
–ly	2. quiet _____
–ful	3. play _____
un–	4. ____ equal
pre–	5. ____ view
over–	6. _____ board
–ly	7. sad _____
–ful	8. dread _____
un–	9. ____ done
pre–	10. ____ wind

Choose five of the new words and write sentences using them.

11. _____

12. _____

13. _____

14. _____

15. _____

Penguins at the Pole

Name	Height (average)	Weight (average)	Interesting Facts
emperor penguin	4 feet	70 pounds	The movie *March of the Penguins* is about emperor penguins.
Adélie penguin	$1\frac{1}{2}$ feet	10 pounds	Adélie penguins were named after the wife of a French naval officer who explored Antarctica.
king penguin	2 feet	30 pounds	King penguins are the second-largest penguins in the world.
chinstrap penguin	2 feet	10 pounds	Chinstrap penguins get their name from the black line of feathers under their chins.
gentoo penguin	$2\frac{1}{2}$ feet	12 pounds	Gentoo penguins are the fastest swimming penguins.

Use the chart to answer the questions.

1. Which penguin is the largest in the world? _____

2. Which penguin is the smallest? _____

3. How tall is the gentoo penguin? _____

4. How much does the chinstrap penguin weigh? _____

5. Which penguin was named after a woman? _____

Antarctica Errors

Circle six things that are wrong in the picture.

A Planet Plan

 Recycle it! You can recycle paper, metal, plastic, and many other things.

 Leg it! For short trips, walk instead of taking a car.

 Bike it! For distances that are too long to walk, consider riding your bike.

 Turn it off! To save electricity, turn off the lights when you leave a room.

 Plant it! Plant something green in your yard or local park.

 Bag it! Take your own bag when you shop. You can save paper and plastic.

Write what the people did. Use the terms above. The first one has been done for you.

1. Miranda buys DVDs. She put them in her backpack instead of a plastic bag. __Bag it!__

2. Carlos and Pete plant flowers at Hiddenwood Park. _____

3. Tina rides her new bike to soccer practice. _____

4. Tyron takes soda cans to the recycling center. _____

5. Kerrie switches off the lights in the kitchen when she is finished making a snack. _____

Earth Endings

April 22 is Earth Day. It is a day to honor the planet. Every year, millions of people "go green" on Earth Day. This means they do things to help the planet. They clean up litter, recycle, and plant trees. TV shows and websites use Earth Day to teach people how to keep our land, air, and water clean.

Earth Day began when a United States senator suggested a day of education about Earth. In 1970, hundreds of college students organized the first Earth Day. About 20 million people celebrated.

Earth Day 1970 taught people about pollution. It also showed people how to save energy. Soon, the United States government made new laws to protect earth. The Clean Air Act of 1970 limited the pollution made by cars and factories. The government also created a special group that works to help the planet. It is called the Environmental Protection Agency.

Write **true** or **false** after each statement about the reading.

1. Earth Day is celebrated on May 22. _____

2. Earth Day is a day to honor the planet. _____

3. To "go green" means to turn into a monster.

_____

4. The Clean Air Act limits the amount of pollution from cars and factories. _____

5. The Environmental Protection Agency protects earth.

_____

Answer Key

Page 6
1. jet
2. pilot
3. wheels
4. on water
5. around the world or many wonderful places

Page 7
4 The family watches a movie.
3 The Andersons get on a plane.
5 Mrs. Anderson likes to fly.
2 Mrs. Anderson is afraid to fly.
1 The Andersons are going to Disneyland.

Page 8
1. January 15, 1929
2. February 22, 1732
3. February 12, 1809
4. Answers will vary.

Page 9

Page 10
1. true
2. false
3. true
4. true

Page 11
1. Cattle eat a lot of grass.
2. Calves can walk soon after they are born.
3. Cattle that work on farms are called oxen.
4. Cattle drink up to 50 gallons of water a day.

Page 12
green dress, black hat, cell phone, dolls, blue dress, books, yellow dress, blue hat, umbrella

Page 13
1. b
2. a
3. a
4. c

Page 14
1. African elephant
2. Asian elephant

Page 15
The following words should be circled: *Animals in Africa, Asian Animals, Tusks and Trunks, Animals*

in Zoos, Big Animals Around the World

Page 16
1. 330
2. swimming, weather, beaches
3. two
4. boat
5. Answers will vary.

Page 17
1, 2, and 4

Page 18

	Island	Country	City	Language
1.	✓			
2.			✓	
3.		✓		
4.				✓

Page 19
1. 10°F
2. Sunday and Monday
3. Tuesday
4. Wednesday, Thursday, Friday, and Saturday
5. winter

Page 20
3 and 4

Page 21
graceful — big
huge — hurt
wounded — smooth
change — jump
bounce — money

Page 22

Main Ideas		Supporting Details
3	kinds of igloos	Igloos are made of blocks of snow.
1	what an igloo is	The smallest igloos are made quickly.
2	who lives in igloos	People did not live in igloos every day.

Page 23

Page 24
1. a
2. b
3. a
4. b

Page 25

Page 26
1. light
2. the mirror
3. The patterns were fun to watch.
4. Answers will vary.

Page 27
The colors may vary but should match on each side.

Page 28
1. S
2. S
3. M
4. S
5. S

Page 29

	Ricky's Tree	Martin's Tree
1.	has limes	doesn't have limes
2.	too small to climb	big enough for climbing
3.	small	big
4.	weak	strong
5.	doesn't have a tree house	has a tree house

Page 30
1. false
2. true
3. false
4. false
5. true

Page 31
1. b
2. b
3. a
4. a
5. b

Page 32
1. land
2. to make
3. patterns
4. surprise
5. unknown

Page 33
1. folktale
2. spider
3. the past
4. spiders
5. after

Page 34
1. Uh-oh
2. Oh, boy
3. oh
4. Oh, yeah

Page 35
1. answers may include: dashed, gobbled, hopped, quickly, splashed, sprinted, threw
2. his mom's purse
3. Answers will vary.
4. Answers will vary.

Page 36
2 People used long metal sticks to write.
3 People discovered that the mineral graphite could make dark marks.
1 People wrote with flat pieces of lead.
4 People put sticks of graphite into wooden tubes.
5 Pencil makers developed a rating system to show hardness.

Page 37
color: colorful, colored
erase: eraser, erased
light: lighter, lightest

Page 38
1. quadruplets
2. quad
3. quadruple
4. quadriceps
5. quad toms

Page 39

	Ned	Luke	Joe	Peter
1.				✓
2.		✓		
3.			✓	
4.	✓			

Page 40
1. a
2. a
3. a
4. b

Page 41
1. fact
2. fact
3. fiction
4. fiction
5. fact

Page 42
1. b
2. a
3. a
4. b

Page 43
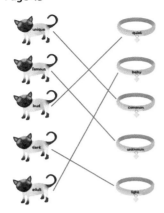

Page 44
1. more than 200 years old
2. Jane Taylor
3. five
4. shining, glowing
5. look through, peek through, shine through

Page 45
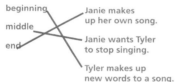
beginning
middle
end

Janie makes up her own song.

Janie wants Tyler to stop singing.

Tyler makes up new words to a song.

Page 46
1. Uno cards
2. Fiat Uno
4. University of New Orleans

Page 47
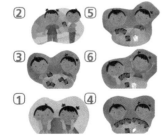

Page 48
1. C, E
2. C, E
3. E, C
4. E, C
5. C, E

Page 49
The following words should be circled: visited, saw, went, watched, drove, slid, rented, rode, having

Page 50
1. a
2. b
3. b
4. a

Page 51
1. wagons, toys, wheels, horses
2. boxes, buses, watches, dresses
3. companies, countries, babies, stories

Page 52

Page 53
1. swimming
2. skiing
3. hiking
4. camping

Page 54
1. more
2. taller
3. warm
4. eat
5. fewer

Page 55
1. plains
2. planes
3. weigh
4. way
5. There
6. their

Page 56
1. a
2. b
3. a
4. a

Page 57
1, 3, and 5

Page 58

	Nickname	Sport	Years played
1.	Air Jordan	basketball	1980s, 1990s
2.	Babe	baseball	1913–1945
3.	Chris	tennis	1972–1989
4.	The Champ	boxing	1960s, 1970s
5.	The Tennessee Tornado	running	1956–1962

Page 59
1. drawing of a boy hitting a baseball at home plate
2. drawing of a girl standing on a diving board
3. drawing of a girl starting a race and the start line

Page 60
1. true
2. false
3. true
4. false
5. false

Page 61
What: A Tea Party
Day: Saturday, March 3
Time: 1:00–3:00 PM
Where: Pine Park
Call: 555-2134

Page 62
1. a
2. b
3. b
4. b
5. a

Page 63
nouns: tricycle, wheel, children, tire
verbs: move, work, ride, learn
adjectives: small, big, tall, easy

Page 64
1. *The Wizard of Oz*
2. *Finding Nemo*
3. *Finding Nemo*
4. *Shrek*
5. Answers will vary.

Page 65

Titles of movies will vary.

Page 66
1. 1
2. 6
3. 8
4. 3
5. Answers will vary.

Page 67
1. Answers may include: ten, tan, true, tune, talk, tear, team, table
2. Answers may include: bag, tag, rag, bug
3. Answers may include: ran, tan, fan, man, van
4. Answers may include: plate, date, gate, eight, skate
5. Answers may include: giant, large, great, tall, jumbo

Page 68

	In 1961	Today
1.	$2.75	$47
2.	$2.25	$29.99
3.	50¢	$15
4.	45¢	about $7
5.	20	More than 100

Page 69

Page 70
1. Golden Gate Bridge
2. Delta Works
3. Chunnel and Itaipu Dam
4. Panama Canal
5. CN Tower and Empire State Building

Page 71
1. seven
2. five
3. six
4. Mexico
5. ten

Page 72
1.-3.
- As I see it, yes ✓
- Ask again later ✓
- Better not tell you now ✓
- Cannot predict now ✓
- Concentrate and ask again ✓
- Don't count on it
- It is certain (circled)
- It is decidedly so (circled)
- Most likely (circled)
- My reply is no
- My sources say no
- Outlook good (circled)
- Outlook not so good
- Reply hazy, try again ✓
- Signs point to yes
- Very doubtful
- Without a doubt (circled)
- Yes (circled)
- Yes–definitely (circled)
- You may rely on it (circled)

4. X above: Abe Bookman
5. Wavy line: magic 8-ball

Page 73
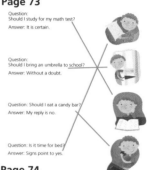
Question: Should I study for my math test?
Answer: It is certain.

Question: Should I bring an umbrella to school?
Answer: Without a doubt.

Question: Should I eat a candy bar?
Answer: My reply is no.

Question: Is it time for bed?
Answer: Signs point to yes.

Page 74
1. false
2. true
3. true
4. false
5. false

Page 75
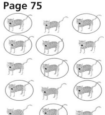

Page 76
1. javelin throw, discus throw, and shot put
2. hurdles, long jump, high jump, pole vault
3. 100-meter run, 400-meter run, 1,500-meter run, 110-meter hurdles

Page 77
Possible answers: cat, hat, hot, dot, cot, not, lot, ten, den, can, tan, con, ton, led, ate, late, hate, hated, ant, the, then, head, lead, deal, teal, ace, lace, laced, lane, cane, one, done, lone, alone, tone, toned, cone, death, decal, noel, hole, dole, coal, tale, told, hold, cold

Page 78
1. 4 and 10
2. 7
3. 5
4. 1 and 11
5. Answers will vary.

Page 79
The following should be circled:
paper, a book, beads, a box, glue, shoelaces, a pot, ribbons, markers, a pencil, scissors

Page 80
1. true
2. true
3. false
4. false
5. false

Page 81
1. A Chicken Lays a Dozen Eggs
2. Dan's Dozens of Cousins
3. A Baker Makes a Cake
4. Martha's Birthday Surprise

Page 82
unlucky/not lucky
story/floor
superstition/belief
popular/well-liked
skip/leave out

Page 83

Page 84
1. a
2. b
3. a
4. b

Page 85
3, 1
6, 4
2, 5

Page 86
1. bass
2. mandolin
3. banjo
4. washboard
5. harmonica

Page 87
1. Answers could include: blow, blast, black, blade, blame, blind, blink, block
2. Answers could include: true, Sue, glue, due
3. Answers could include: blueberries, car, sky, shirt, shoes
4. Answers could include: blueprint, bluebird, bluebell
5. Answers could include: few, cue, knew, true

Page 88

Page 89
1. b
2. b
3. a
4. b

Page 90
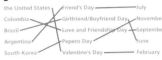

Page 91
Answers will vary.

Page 92
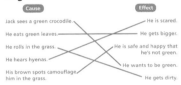

Page 93
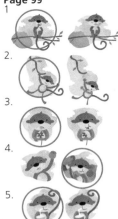

Page 94
1. metal
2. water
3. machines
4. cold
5. animals

Page 95
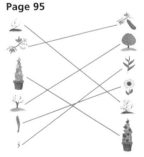

Page 96
1. Orange, Ohio
2. Orange, California
3. Orange, Texas
4. Orange, New York
5. Orange City, Florida

Page 97
1. girl
2. three
3. four
4. Aren't you

Page 98
1, 8, 3
4, 5, 6
7, 2, 9

Page 99
1
2.
3.
4.
5.

Page 100
1. a
2. b
3. a
4. b

Page 101

	Bertha	Bruce
1.		✓
2.	✓	✓
3.	✓	
4.		✓
5.	✓	✓

Page 102
orbit/go around
enormous/very big
sphere/ball
provides/gives
depends on/needs

Page 103
1. FELLOW
2. FELL
3. BELL
4. BELLY
5. YELL

Page 104
1. false
2. true
3. false
4. false
5. true

Page 105
Stories will vary.

Page 106
1. purple onion
2. eggplant
3. plum
4. purple potato
5. grapes
6. blackberries

Page 107
Grains: oatmeal, bread
Vegetable: corn, green beans
Fruit: grapes, strawberries, bananas
Milk: milk
Meat: chicken, pork chops

Page 108
1. S, S, M
2. M, S, S
3. S, S, M
4. S, M, S

Page 109
1. Alaska
2. brownies
3. fish and berries
4. brownie mix
5. berries

Page 110
The following should be circled:
television, radio, videogame, lamp, air conditioner, computer

Page 111
1. Answers may include: brush, branch, brook, bright
2. Answers may include: bears, monkeys, dogs, deer
3. Answers may include: town, gown, down, frown
4. Answers may include: bread, cookies, potatoes, meat

Page 112
1. black belt
2. black diamond
3. Blackberry
4. blackout
5. blackboard

Page 113
The following should be underlined: bluebirds, farmhouse, afternoon, rainbow

Page 114
1. opinion
2. fact
3. fact
4. opinion
5. fact
6. opinion

Page 115
1. notebook, bookshelf
2. sunlight, lighthouse
3. blackout, outside
4. homework, workout

Page 116
1. 82
2. mountains, forests, rivers
3. straight
4. New York City
5. 1946

Page 117

Page 118
1. GPS
2. cellular phone
3. MLU
4. GPS

Page 119
1. false
2. true
3. false
4. false
5. true

Page 120
1. =
2. >
3. >
4. >
5. <
6. =

Page 121
_4_ Farah and her class went back to the bus.
_2_ She watched a video about the White House.
_5_ She flipped a coin with Jack.
_1_ Farah went to Washington, D.C., with her class.
_3_ She saw an old map in the Map Room.

Page 122
1. weapons
2. pie
3. tins
4. plastic
5. 50

Page 123

Page 124
1. true
2. false
3. true
4. false

Page 125

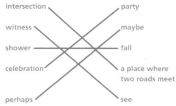

Page 126
1. in the Atlantic Ocean
2. 1918
3. hurricanes
4. scientists

Page 127
un-: explained, believable
mis-: take, understood, place
dis-: honest, agree, appear

Page 128

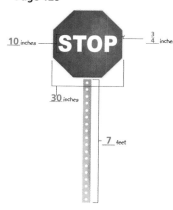

Page 129
Answers may include:
Two-letter words: to, an, at, on, as, go, so, no
Three-letter words: tag, nag, sag, con, ton, son, tan, can, act, oat, sat, cat, not, got, cot, gas
Four-letter words: tags, nags, cons, tons, tans, acts, oats, cats, cots, goat, coat, snag, cost, gnat, song, sang

Page 130

Pyramid	Country	Fact
Great Pyramid of Giza	Egypt	used to be 485 ft. high
Great Pyramid of Cholula	Mexico	has five miles of tunnels
Pyramid of the Sun	Mexico	has steps going up the sides
Pyramid of Cestius	Italy	has paintings on the wall

Page 131
Words should be added in this order: Mexico, Sun, huge, inside, outside, Spanish, sunny

Page 132

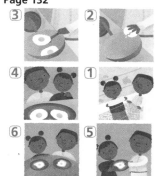
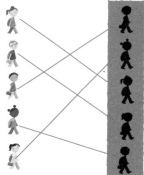

Page 133
1. Sunny
2. a house
3. funny

Page 134
lizards, a lot of rain, plants, birds, trees

Page 135
All of Jeremy's friends wanted an Umbrehat.

Page 136
1. N
2. F
3. N
4. N
5. F
6. N

Page 137

Page 138
1. true
2. true
3. false
4. false
5. false

Page 139

Page 140
1. ice and flavored syrup
2. Samuel Bert
3. 1920
4. by hand or with a blender
5. at sporting events, fairs, carnivals, circuses, ice-cream trucks

Page 141
Drawings will vary.

Page 142
1. Paint
2. Cut
3. Fold
4. Tie
5. Hang

Page 143
1. bead, through, string,
2. scissors, under, inside
3. instructions

Page 144
1. face the music
2. head of state
3. Two heads are better than one
4. face-to-face
5. heads or tails

Page 145
1. do fun things
2. fictional events
3. Don's and Louisa's
4. a side of a coin

Page 146

Animal	Quick Fact
earthworms	have cells that sense light
owls	can't move their eyes
chameleons	eyes move in different directions
bats	are color-blind
spiders	some live in caves and don't need eyes

Page 147
Louis Braille

Page 148
1 and 3

Page 149

Page 150
Answers may include:
-ear: appear, dear, fear, gear, hear, near, rear, tear, year
-ere: adhere, here, mere, severe, sphere, we're
-eer: deer, cheer, engineer, sheer, steer

Page 151
1. a snoop
2. listen secretly
3. kneeled down
4. very happy
5. ruined

Page 152

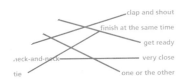

- clap and shout
- finish at the same time
- get ready
- very close
- one or the other

neck-and-neck

tie

Page 156
1. North America and South America
2. hide or dig a hole
3. 4 feet
4. they fill their stomachs with air
5. six minutes

Page 157
1. colorful
2. higher
3. comfortable
4. fastest
5. careful
6. wooden

Page 158
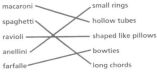

macaroni — small rings
spaghetti — hollow tubes
ravioli — shaped like pillows
anellini — bowties
farfalle — long chords

Page 159
1. brothers
2. elbows
3. saying
4. sisters
5. own

Page 160
1. Europe
2. writing
3. hobby
4. calligraphy
5. thousands

Page 161
1. writing by hand
2. teacher
3. likes computers
4. stop using a computer

Page 162
1. false
2. false
3. true
4. false
5. true

Page 163
1. a
2. b
3. a
4. b

Page 164
1. Circled: armadillos, cattle, sheep, worms
2. Underlined: stomach, heart, lungs, brain
3. Wavy line: digest, break down food
4. X above: inflate
5. Two lines under: grumbling

Page 165
1. Julie
2. four
3. her mom
4. her dad
5. Answers will vary.

Page 166
1. leg it
2. Shake a leg
3. last leg
4. Break a leg
5. pull your leg

Page 167
1. carnival
2. bag
3. seems
4. rest
5. in front

Page 168
1. camels
2. flamingos
3. elephants
4. cattle
5. crickets

Page 169
Answers may include:
K: kneel, kneeling, knit, know, knew, knife, knock, knob
B: climb, lamb, comb, dumb, bomb, doubt, crumb, tomb,
H: ache, hour, anchor, character, school, orchid, rhyme, whale, where, when, wheel, what, whistle, white
W: wrinkle, write, wrote, whole, wreck, wrench, wrestle, wrap, wrong, who, sword

Page 170
1. 12
2. 3
3. 6
4. 5,280
5. the United States

Page 171

foot — stand
hand — stroke
ear — glasses
back — ball
eye — ache

Page 172
1. Circled: Mediterranean and Red
2. Underlined: Atlantic, Indian
3. X above: Lake Victoria, Lake Tanganyika
4. Wavy line under: Africa
5. Check mark above: Nile

Page 173
Stories will vary.

Page 174
1. smallest
2. about
3. Queen
4. 3
5. biggest

Page 175

Page 176
1. no
2. yes
3. no
4. no
5. yes

Page 177
Places: the outback, Sydney, Lake Mackay
Animals: koala bear, crocodile, dingo
Plants and flowers: water lily, eucalyptus tree, orchid

Page 178
1. Mount Everest
2. K2
3. Kanchenjunga
4. Lhotse
5. Makalu

Page 179
2, 3, and 5

Page 180
1. true
2. true
3. false
4. true
5. false

Page 181
1. a bird and a coyote
2. a lake
3. why bluebirds are blue and coyotes are brown
4. don't brag
5. Answers will vary.

Page 182
1. panpipes
2. cajón
3. charango
4. ocarina
5. maracas

Page 183
1. overlook
2. quietly
3. playful
4. unequal
5. preview
6. overboard

7. sadly
8. dreadful
9. undone
10. rewind
11.-15. Sentences will vary.

Page 184
1. emperor penguin
2. Adélie penguin
3. $2\frac{1}{2}$ feet tall
4. 10 pounds
5. Adélie penguin

Page 185

Page 186
2. Plant it!
3. Bike it!
4. Recycle it!
5. Turn it off!

Page 187
1. false
2. true
3. false
4. true
5. true